A THINKER'S GUIDE TO LIVING WELL

A THINKER'S GUIDE TO LIVING WELL

Dennis E. Bradford

Open Court
La Salle, Illinois

Cover illustration: 'Contentment' by Maxfield Parrish,
oil on masonite, 1927.

OPEN COURT and the above logo are registered in the U.S. Patent
and Trademark Office
©1990 by Open Court Publishing Company

First printing 1990

Printed and bound in the United States of America.

Library of Congress Cataloging-in-Publication Data

Bradford, Dennis E.

    A thinker's guide to living well / Dennis E. Bradford.
        p.   cm.
    Includes bibliographical references and index.
    ISBN 0-8126-9138-5. — ISBN 0-8126-9139-3 (pbk.)
      1. Life skills—North America—Handbooks, manuals, etc.
2. Quality of life—North America—Handbooks, manuals, etc.
I. Title.
HQ2039.N7B73 1990   90-41070
306—dc20   CIP

To Laura

Contents

Acknowledgements

I thank my colleagues in the Department of Philosophy for shouldering my teaching burden during the fall semester, 1985, and the State University of New York for granting me a sabbatical leave that semester. I thank Pamela Thomas for her typing. I thank my father Brian K. Bradford for his comments on the Appendix and Chapters 2, 3, and 4. I thank my colleague Walter Soffer for his comments on Chapter 6. I thank my mentor Panayot Butchvarov, my colleague Gary Cox, my wife Laura Bradford, my mother Ethel Bradford, and David Ramsay Steele of Open Court for their comments on various parts of the whole manuscript. Most importantly, I thank my friend Terry Kent for his comments on the whole manuscript. Of course, I alone am responsible for any remaining errors.

Homo sum, et nihil humanum a me alienum puto.

— TERENCE

1

Introduction

Benjamin Franklin had it right. He wrote in his *Autobiography* that "When I disengag'd myself . . . from private Business, I flatter'd myself that by the sufficient tho' moderate Fortune I had acquir'd, I had secur'd Leisure during the rest of my Life, for Philosophical [scientific] Studies and Amusements".[1] Franklin did not inherit his wealth: he made himself wealthy. How? He learned the technical skill of printing, opened his own printing business, made it successful, and sold it. Franklin did not go through the bother of becoming wealthy simply for the purpose of being wealthy. He wanted to become wealthy to devote more time to his projects—his inventions, his scientific achievement in advancing the theoretical understanding of electricity, and his important public service. The idea of living well is the idea of doing and faring well; Franklin's story is the story of a person who did and fared well.

He himself realized that he wouldn't have succeeded without ability, hard work, and a good plan. "I have always thought that one Man of tolerable Abilities may work great Changes, and accomplish great Affairs among Mankind, if he first forms a good Plan, and, cutting off all Amusements or other Employments that would divert his Attention, makes the Execution of that same Plan his sole Study and Business".[2] Notice that he claims that a person of "tolerable" abilities may have "great" success. A person of average abilities may do and fare well. So it is not lack of ability that keeps many of us back.

Nor is it lack of effort. Of course, a lazy person is unlikely to do well. Franklin himself emphasized hard work: he tried, he tells us, to instruct "the common People" to work harder by interlarding the calendar days in his almanacs "with Proverbial Sentences, chiefly such as inculcated Industry and Frugality, as the Means of procuring Wealth and thereby securing Virtue, it being more difficult for a Man in Want to act always honestly".[3] But many people work hard without either doing or faring very well: think of the hundreds of millions of peasants and laborers who toil hour after hour, day after day, year after year, decade after decade, without seeming to improve their lot. Some work hard and make it; some work hard and don't. So some toil is more productive than other toil. We, today, in North America are blessed with a fruitful economic structure. For this reason, all things being equal, the toil of North Americans is likely to be more productive than that of Africans or Indians or Chinese. Nevertheless, even many average North Americans who work hard don't seem to improve their lot. Why is that? The reason such persons cannot avoid frittering away the products of their hard work is usually their lack of a good plan. They may have great understanding about many specific areas of life, but they often seem to lack an overall understanding of where they are going or what they want to do when they get there. What is required is the ability to put it all together—not the ability to be successful in a single aspect of life.

Providing a good plan that works is what this book is all about. With a good plan it is possible for the average North American who works at it to do well.

I do not claim that this plan is original with me. I have already indicated that it is at least as old as Franklin. It would be extraordinary if I were somehow the first human being in history to develop a defensible plan for living life well. Nor do I claim that the only way to become wise is by following this plan. This becomes obvious as soon as one considers other wise men—especially those who lived outside our economic environment, such as Confucius or Socrates, or those who had extraordinary abilities, such as Aristotle or Shakespeare. I do not even claim to be wise myself. Parts of this plan will not work outside the economic environment of present-day North America.

What I claim is simply that an industrious person of average abilities who follows the plan in this book will do better in life.

The basic idea is that it is possible to learn how to become healthier, wealthier, and wiser and that health may be a means to wealth and that wealth may be a means to wisdom. Everyone knows what it is to be healthy and wealthy. But some may fear the idea of being wise. There is nothing to fear. It should not conjure up an image of a hermit meditating on some Himalayan mountaintop. It should simply stimulate thoughts about life lived well, about a successful life, about a life filled with rewarding work and lasting pleasures, about a life made of consistently excellent decisions. Tranquillity, peace of mind, is a by-product of such a life.

This book is like a cookbook. The author of a cookbook does not say, for example, 'Follow this recipe for making

delicious lentil soup.' We are not given categorical imperatives; we are given hypothetical imperatives. 'If you want to
make a delicious lentil soup, follow this recipe.' Similarly,
anyone seriously interested in becoming healthier, wealthier,
or wiser may want to consider implementing my suggestions.

It is possible to be wise without either being healthy or
being wealthy. But surely it is preferable to be all three—just
ask anyone who is either unhealthy or poor.

We always tend to follow the pathways of our own
expectations. Part of being wise is having realistic expectations. Let us begin by thinking about what we may expect
with regard to our own health and by trying to understand
how, as laymen, we may become as healthy as possible.
Here, because of advances in medical science, we have a
definite advantage over Franklin.

2

Health

We are our bodies. It is not as if we are, say, immaterial ghosts trapped within bodily machines. Notice that we ordinarily identify ourselves with our bodies. Just think, for example, of the natural response to the question, 'Where's the Pope?' 'He's in the Vatican.' We take the Pope to be his body. And we do this not just in the third-person (namely, he, she, or it) but also in the first-person (namely, I). For example, if my neighbor comes over to my house and calls out 'Where are you?', I might well answer, 'I'm in the basement.' I would never think or say something like, 'My body is in the basement!' Or, if I decline someone's invitation to go for a walk, I might explain by saying that I'm not feeling well today; I would not say that my body is not feeling well today. Of course, this may not accurately represent our ordinary understanding or our ordinary understanding may be inadequate. But I deny that, in this case, it is.

The chief motivation for denying the claim that we are our bodies may come from the fear that death is annihilation. Either death is something or it is nothing. If it is nothing, life is meaningless. Hence, death must be something. But, if so, what could it be? The best answer that anyone has ever proposed is that death is the separation of mind (or soul) and body: one's body dies but one's mind lives on. So, according to this way of thinking, we are here and now two things: a nonphysical mind and a physical body.

But there are several things wrong with this way of thinking. First, as Epicurus pointed out long ago, there is no good reason to fear death if death is nothing. It is rational to fear something if that thing could be painful, but how could death be painful if it is nothing? Each of us has a good reason to fear *dying* painfully, but there is no good reason to fear *being dead* painfully because the idea of being dead painfully is incoherent. If this is correct, then there is no good reason to make up some theory that attempts to postulate how death can be something. Second, which object is my mind? As Hume pointed out, it is not so easy to answer this question. And, assuming for the moment that each of us has a nonphysical mind, is it the same enduring thing that changes? I am suspicious of the claim that it is.[4] Third, continuing the assumption, how are we to understand the connection between the mind and the body? The answer here depends upon the answer to the second question. I may, of course, be wrong, but I don't think that there are any satisfactory answers to either question. Fourth, why assume that life is meaningless if death is annihilation? Not only do I think that there is no satisfactory answer to this question, but I also think that life is *more* likely to be mean-ingful if death is annihilation. Although I return to the question about the meaning of life in Chapter 9, this work is not the place for a thorough discussion of these issues. Fifth, it is false that I am here and now a mysterious union of two radically different kinds of substances: I am one person. Aren't you?

If we are our bodies, it follows that to value yourself is to value your body. There is no difference. Should we value ourselves/our bodies? Should we value our lives?

It seems obvious to me that life is good (valuable). Though, of course, they might all have been mistaken, no significant thinker has ever believed that it isn't. What is good for our bodies is good. If this is mistaken, there is no point in being further concerned with what is good for our bodies.

But how are we to know what is good for our bodies? The natural assumption is that, if I feel good physically, my body is in good condition. Feeling good (in this case) is feeling pleasant or feeling pleasurable; feeling bad is being, to some degree, in pain. Are pleasure and pain reliable guides to the condition of our bodies?

Often they are good guides. But they are not *necessarily* good guides. It is possible, for example, to feel good and yet not to be healthy. So, even if it is true that feeling good usually goes with being healthy, it is not necessarily true. And it is possible to feel pain and yet not be in a state of ill health. So, even if it is true that feeling bad usually goes with being in ill health, it is not necessarily true. Consider some examples.

Descartes, the father of modern philosophy, like Aristotle, mentions in this context the case of a person suffering from dropsy.[5] One who is in ill health because of dropsy suffers dryness of the throat and this leads naturally to the painful state of being thirsty. But such a person does not need a drink, which shows how the natural bodily feeling is corrupt in this case. Or consider the case of a healthy athlete. Such a person may not be thirsty after exercising hard on a hot day and drinking some water, and yet he (or, of course, she) may need more water. Since he needs more water than he has taken in, there ought to be a feeling of thirst—but there isn't. Or consider the case of a heroin addict who may desperately want another dose of heroin; such a person ought not to do what his body seems to instruct him to do. Or consider the case of a cigarette smoker who needs a cigarette after dinner. Or consider the case of an alcoholic who needs a drink upon arising in the morning. Or consider someone in the early stages of leukemia who feels fine. (Notice how natural it is to proceed from the idea of health to the idea of health-related habits such as smoking, drinking, exercising, and so on. I consider such habits in the next three chapters.)

A body in good condition is a whole body that is healthy. The idea of being healthy is the idea of being free from disease, the symptoms of disease, or injury. If the previous argument is a good one, the idea of a healthy body does not necessarily correspond to a feeling of pleasure and the idea of an unhealthy body does not necessarily correspond to a feeling of pain.

1. Since your bodily feelings do not necessarily give you an accurate assessment of your health, how should you gain an accurate assessment of your health? 2. And what, if anything, can you do about your health? 3. And what, if something can be done, should you do about your health?

1. An accurate assessment of your health depends upon understanding the state of your body. This calls for an expert diagnosis. Fortunately, in this field there are experts. Like most people, I am not an expert in this field and, so, must choose among experts without having the expertise to guarantee a good choice. If you are in a similar situation you may benefit from trying to understand and to evaluate the following argument. If my argument is sound, my conclusions are true.

If it is unsound (in other words, if my reasoning is poor [invalid] or if at least one of my initial beliefs [premisses] is false), then my conclusions may be ignored because they may be false. It is offered as a beginning—not as the last word.

The basic problem here is finding an expert. The following is meant for nonexperts. It is intended as an example of how to go about harnessing the understanding of others and making it work in your own favor.

There are *two steps* in the process. i. *Making an appointment.* ii. *Evaluating the performance of the expert whom you have chosen.* If the expert turns out to be not so expert after all, the process should be repeated.

i. The goal of medical science is better health for humans; its subject matter is the prevention and cure of diseases. The method of medical science is the free and open discussion of rational beliefs concerning its subject matter.[6] The relevant expert is a good physician. You ought to acquire the services of a good, primary care (in other words, first contact care) physician. Of course, the quality of the evaluation that you eventually receive will depend upon the limits of the present development of medical science and the competence of the selected individual. You can do nothing about the present development of medical science, but you are able to make it more likely that the physician you select will be a good one.

It should be admitted at the outset that it is possible for a nonphysician to make a state-of-the-art evaluation of your health. But it is unlikely. It is far more likely that you will get a better evaluation from someone who has what are reasonably regarded as the best credentials. What, then, are the best credentials?

There are a number of different kinds of doctors recog-

9

nized by law: doctors of medicine, doctors of osteopathy, doctors of chiropractic, dentists, optometrists, podiatrists, and doctors of philosophy. The latter four kinds are obviously irrelevant. The chief idea governing the theory of chiropractic is that all disease is caused by misalignments of the spine, but that belief is false. The germ theory of disease is well established. If so, though you might wish to visit a doctor of chiropractic for a massage, you should not select a doctor of chiropractic as the expert to evaluate the state of your health. That leaves doctors of medicine and doctors of osteopathy.

With respect to osteopaths, the State of California, for example, does not recognize any difference between them and doctors of medicine. Some excellent medical schools have osteopaths as faculty members and some osteopaths are extremely competent in their areas of expertise. Some osteopaths are certified by such medical boards as the American Board of Internal Medicine. Even if it may be true that osteopathic schools are generally inferior to medical schools, it may also be true that there are nevertheless outstanding students who attend them and go on to become outstanding physicians.

With respect to doctors of medicine, there are general practitioners, self-designated specialists, and certified specialists. Depending upon the program, a student may take six to eight years after high school to complete the college and medical school courses necessary to obtain an M.D. (Doctor of Medicine). A new M.D. must complete one year of approved postgraduate training (called 'PGY-1' or 'internship') prior to taking the state board examination for medical licensure. A general practitioner needs no further formal training. A self-designated specialist is simply a general practitioner who has chosen to pinpoint his practice in a certain area of medical care. A certified specialist is a medical doctor who has passed a specialty board examination; qualification for these exams involves spending an additional two to five years, depending upon the specialty, in advanced hospital training as residents. Of the 66 different specialties, the one that is probably most relevant is internal medicine, because it deals with the prevention, diagnosis, and treatment of nonsurgical diseases. (Some board-certified internists have also become Fellows of the American College of Physicians [F.A.C.P.].) It does not seem unreasonable to select as a well qualified expert, then, a board-certified internist. An internist who is a Fellow of the American College of Physicians will be board-certified.

My recommendation, then, is that, on paper at least, the best sort of physician would be a board-certified internist. Even if this is true, it is not a recommendation that should be unthinkingly followed. For example, it is likely that there are board-certified internists who could not give you a state-of-the-art physical examination (perhaps because they specialize in some other area of medicine) and it is certainly the case that there are physicians who are not board-certified internists (for example, family practitioners) who are able to give you such a physical. You are simply looking for a well-qualified, primary care physician who is interested in doing physical examinations and who is competent enough to do them well.

Often the best medical minds are found in university medical centers. And many medical school professors supplement their incomes by practicing privately. (Many medical school professors volunteer their services to the medical school.) If you are interested in selecting a primary care physician you might do well to contact the nearest teaching hospital and to try to locate a professor who is an internist willing to take on new patients. He should be either a board-certified internist (who has passed the American specialty board examination) or a board-eligible internist (who has finished the required postgraduate training, but either has not yet been in practice for two years, which is the minimum amount of time required before taking the certifying examination, or who has not passed the board examination [find out which]). Failing that, a medical school professor might have a good recommendation or two concerning local physicians. Or you might try contacting the nearest large medical center or the local community hospital with the best reputation. In some com-munities there are local medical societies or public interest groups that provide lists of doctors' names, addresses, and specialties. And don't overlook the yellow pages. Either the listing itself or the physician's secretary will be able to provide information on whether or not that particular physician is a board-certified internist.

Any information gleaned from friends, relatives, or neighbors about physicians is not likely to be reliable except concerning physicians' personalities. A much more reliable guide is a medical directory. Your local library should have a copy of one such as the *Directory of Medical Specialists*, which is published for the American Board of Medical Specialties. Such a guide should indicate which medical school a physician attended; ensure, at least, that it is fully accredited. It should indicate where the physician did postgraduate training or residency; the best such programs tend to be in large, well-known teaching hospitals. It should indicate whether or not the physician is board-certified. It should indicate the physician's hospital appointments; these are important because the best hospitals screen physicians carefully before appointment and periodically re-evaluate the physicians on their staffs.

There are other factors to consider in addition to a physician's credentials. Where is the physician's office? It should be either near available public transportation or within a relatively short drive and have sufficient parking. The hospital with which that physician is affiliated should not be too far away. Who covers for him when he is not on call? Are his office fees affordable? Is he willing to make essential housecalls and to go to the hospital emergency room if you are admitted there? Is his office neat and clean? Is his staff efficient at answering the phone and keeping records? Are they friendly and helpful?

And there are several personal factors to consider. Is a physician's sex important to you? If so, choose accordingly. A physician's age may be important. A younger physician may be more up to date than an older physician, but an older physician may have more clinical experience. Are you comfortable with this physician's personality? You should be able to tell after a brief interview. Does this physician listen carefully? Does he emphasize preventive medicine? Does he explain alternatives clearly? If you have a medical problem beyond his competence, is he likely to refer you willingly to a specialist? Is he informative about what you can expect? Is he available on the phone when you need him? Is he tolerant of your differences with him?[7]

The point is to locate the best-qualified physician you are able to and to make an appointment for a complete physical examination to assess your health. Don't expect to locate a perfect physician: there is no such animal. But we in North

13

America today have an abundance of well-qualified physicians and, with a bit of effort, it should be possible for you to locate a suitable one who is willing to take you on.

It's a good idea to try your best to be the best patient your physician has ever had. It is important to do the little things correctly. For example, be prompt for your appointment. And be in good condition for your appointment. Be clean and do not empty your bladder just before your exam since you will be asked to provide a urine sample. When you receive your bill, ensure that it is paid promptly. If you have any complaints about your health, jot them down before your appointment so that you don't forget to mention them. And, if your physician gives you any instructions, follow them exactly. If, for example, the physician instructs you to take a certain amount of medicine in a certain way, take it just that way.

The most important preparatory task is to get yourself in the right state of mind. Realize that it is you, and you alone, who are responsible for those aspects of your health that can be controlled. Your physician is your assistant. Being a good patient does not mean turning over all responsibility to your physician; it does not mean being utterly passive. For example, a good patient tries to understand the basics of preventive medicine. A good patient tries to learn about the basics of medical science by reading and asking questions. A good patient asks questions if he does not understand something that his physician has said. A good patient takes all appropriate preventive measures (see the next three chapters).

Permit me a word about conduct and attitude in the physician's office. If you are an adult and your physician addresses you by your first name, there is no good reason not to address him by his first name. There is no reason to be intimidated: in the presence of a physician you are not in the presence of a god. Your physician should be friendly, courteous, and willing to answer briefly your relevant questions. On the other hand, do not expect your physician to chat with you leisurely; if you have chosen well, your physician is likely to be quite busy. It is most important to listen: you are paying for an expert's evaluation and the only way that you will get the full benefit of it is to listen carefully. If you are asked to do something, do it. In other words, you are likely to get the most for your time and money if you cooperate. And don't be annoyed if you are left alone for periods of time. Expect it: your physician's office is probably not perfectly organized. Take along an interesting magazine.

ii. When the physician whom you have selected examines you, you should examine the physician. The best way to do that is to evaluate the quality of the physical examination that you are given. The only way to do that is to know something about what constitutes a good exam. Your assessment of the quality of the exam that you receive will largely determine whether or not you ever again go back to that particular physician. A superficial, haphazard exam is a waste of time and money.

Different patients are given different exams. One obvious reason for this is that patients differ: in age, in weight, in genetic make-up, and so on. Another reason is that physicians differ. For example, they differ in the amount of importance that they give to certain test results and, as a result, one physician might routinely order a certain test and another might order it only infrequently. Another factor is cost. A certain test might cost hundreds of dollars to administer. If the results of that test are only slightly better than the results of a much less expensive test, a physician might order the more expensive test for a company president who is in a high risk group and whose company is paying for the cost of the exam and might order the less expensive test for a younger, leaner, fitter college student who is in a low risk group and who is paying for her own exam.

Nevertheless, comprehensive physical examinations have many features in common. There is a list of those features in the Appendix; there is no reason to go over it until just before, and just after, your exam. But it is important to remember that it is there and to use it; otherwise, you are less likely to make a good evaluation of your physician's physical examination of you.

Suppose, now, that you have obtained the results of a comprehensive physical examination. Remember that this is an informed opinion by a fallible human being; it may not be accurate. You may be told that you are in excellent health and likely to live to be 120—and you may drop dead tomorrow. Or you may be told that you will likely be dead within three months—and you may live for ten more years. The expert's judgment about the state of your health is superior to your own—but it, too, is fallible.

2. Depending upon the results of your exam, there may or may not be anything that you can do to improve your health. Usually, there will be steps that can be taken—and the next three chapters may be of great use to you. But it must be admitted that, sometimes, nothing can be done; it may be that it is too late for any improvements in your health habits to have any effect.

Even in this extreme case, however, the exam itself can

have a beneficial effect. Regardless of its results, you have come to understand yourself better. Vague illusions or anxieties have been replaced by realistic expectations. Isn't it wise to replace unrealistic ideas by realistic ones? Self understanding is a good. One of the best ways to live well is always to try to live without regrets. You may already have some disease that will kill you. But as you are dying from that disease you will at least have the comfort of knowing that you finally made the best use of the resources at your command, that you hired the best expert you were able to find to conduct the best examination that he could conduct. His understanding may have failed him. Perhaps he was unable to detect your disease early enough to cure it or it is not a curable disease. But at least you gave it your best shot; at least you cannot have any regrets about that. And, along the way, you probably learned a few things about the contemporary practice of medicine.

You have probably removed any anxiety about the state of your health. Either your anxiety was alleviated because you have discovered that you are basically healthy or your anxiety has turned to fear because you have discovered that you have a certain disease or the likelihood of getting a certain disease. But with your fear realistically focussed on a problem, there may be steps that you can take to solve or alleviate that problem. And, even if there are not, you have understood your world better. Whatever decisions you make in the future are likely to be better ones because they are based upon reality and not upon illusion. In this sense, the most valuable result of your physical examination may be the tranquility that comes from a better matching between your beliefs about reality and reality itself.

3. Being healthy is not the purpose of human life. But

health is a good; it is valuable. And it is a means to other goods. If your health is good, you can take steps to preserve it. If your health is poor, you can take whatever reasonable steps you are able to take to improve it—or at least to ensure that it doesn't deteriorate faster than necessary. Of course, not everything about your body is within your control; you do not choose, for example, to be infected by certain viruses or bacteria. But you may be able to take steps that can greatly improve your chances of being healthy. Here are five suggestions.

One of the best steps is a regular, comprehensive physical examination. If you are under 30, you should have a physical examination every three years unless there is some medical abnormality that requires more frequent monitoring. (At least one resting ECG should be taken during this time for use as a reference in future years.) If you are between 30 and 35, exams should be every two years. If you are between 35 and 40, exams should be every 18 months. If you are over 40, exams should be every 12 to 18 months.[8]

A second important step is to make certain that you have had the appropriate immunizations. Vaccines have been developed that are generally effective against a growing list of diseases such as smallpox (which has now actually been eliminated), poliomyelitis, cholera, malaria, plague, pneumococcus, rabies, yellow fever, typhoid, typhus, measles and German measles (rubella), mumps, hepatitis B, tetanus, diphtheria, whooping cough, and influenza. It is true that there is no perfect, risk-free vaccine. At some point, as a program of immunization becomes more and more successful against a certain disease, it becomes more likely that the vaccine itself will cause a greater incidence of illness than the target disease. Nevertheless, people, especially adults, should be immunized. The odds of our becoming diseased if we are not immunized usually speak in favor of immunization. Furthermore, as communal animals, a good case can be made that it is our duty to our community to ensure that we are immunized. Your immunization schedule should be discussed with your physician and your vaccinations should be brought up to date. Normal, adult North Americans who do not travel may only require an occasional tetanus and diphtheria booster. Persons who travel outside North America may require additional immunizations. Annual flu immunizations are recommended for persons in high risk groups (for example, age 65 or older persons, persons with pneumonia, or persons who are severely ill with other diseases). Certain other immunizations are recommended for persons in certain risk groups.

A third important step is to make a reasonable effort to keep up your understanding of major developments in the field of health care. This is an exciting time in the growth of medical understanding, and there is every reason to expect development. For example, there are about 3,000 known genetic diseases. For some of them, symptoms can be alleviated (for example, insulin administration in diabetes, blood transfusions in Cooley's anemia, and diet therapy in phenylketonuria). But no genetic disease can now be cured. However, there have been fascinating recent developments in molecular biology: researchers are busy studying, mapping, and cloning the thousands of human genes in an effort to understand the functioning of a normal body at the molecular level. Once this is understood, gene therapy will be theoretically possible. It should be possible to insert a normal gene into the cells of a patient with a defective gene. (The first successful gene therapy in a mammal was reported in 1984.) This is a wonderful possibility—and a cause of hope for many affected persons. But how can you keep up with such advances?

I have found two publications that are a good first step. One is *The Harvard Medical School Health Letter*, which is exactly what it claims to be, namely, "A Publication for the General Readership, Designed to Provide Accurate and Timely Health Information". The other is the *University of California, Berkeley, Wellness Letter*, which is also exactly what it claims to be, namely, a "newsletter of nutrition, fitness, and stress management" that is published in association with the School of Public Health. Each publication provides short, intelligible, accurate, and current health-related articles. And the *Wellness Letter* in particular is very good at suggesting sources of more information. You need not subscribe to these publications if they are available in a local library. On the other hand, they are relatively inexpensive and it is very convenient if they are delivered to your door. A number of other medical schools throughout North America also publish such medical newsletters.

There are other good sources of general information. Since most people recognize the value of being healthy, there are usually best-selling, health-related books available in bookstores. Unfortunately, many of them, particularly diet books, are of little or no value. It would be wise to ask your physician for advice on this matter. I ask my father. He majored in chemistry and biology at Princeton as an undergraduate, graduated from Columbia Medical School, completed his residency in internal medicine at New York City's Bellevue

Hospital, is a Fellow of the American College of Physicians, has been on the faculty of two different medical schools, and has been in private practice for nearly four decades. I am inclined to take his health-related advice seriously. He highly recommends the Harvard and Berkeley publications mentioned in the previous paragraph.

If you wish to read about some particular area of medicine, ask your physician for advice. For example, if you are arthritic, he may well recom-mend Kate Lorig's and James F. Fries's excellent *Arthritis Helpbook*. Or, depending in part upon your motivation and educational background, he may send you to your local library to look up an article in the current edition of some standard medical textbook. You may even wish to begin regularly perusing a medical journal or two. Currently, accord-ing to my father, the best two are *The New England Journal of Medicine* and the *Journal of the American Medical Association*. Even though it is often possible to get the gist of articles in such places, however, the nonspecialist simply lacks the educational background to evaluate their arguments, which is an excellent reason for relying on the advice of your physician in the first place.

There are also general science periodicals that can help to fill in the gaps in your own scientific background and that are helpful in keeping informed about current developments. One of the best of these is *Scientific American*. But the problem with it is that it takes a good deal of time to read each issue thoroughly. For this reason, I prefer the less detailed science periodical *Science News*. Some of the medical columnists in your local newspaper may be outstanding, and some physicians, for example, Dean Edell, who regularly appear on radio and television are outstanding.

A fourth important step is becoming prepared for health-related emergencies. Everyone should enroll in a Boy Scout or Red Cross or local college course in first aid (to include cardiopulmonary resuscitation and the Heimlich maneuver). It costs little in time and money and, should an emergency occur, you may well be able to save a life—perhaps even your own.

If you are planning a trip abroad, it would be wise to discuss your travel plans in advance with your physician. You should want to know, for each location, which people to contact or which places to go to in order to obtain good medical care. Your physician may well be able to make some recommendations about this. Furthermore, your physician may suggest that you carry a few medical supplies with you as you travel. He may prescribe medication (in advance) for pain, fever, diarrhea, acute upper respiratory infection, and so on. One reason for this is that in many foreign countries dangerous drugs are available over the counter. Your physician may advise you concerning which drugs to get, if needed, and which drugs to avoid. He may be able to advise you on the best way to locate an English-speaking physician. Anyone who travels abroad frequently may wish to consider joining the International Association for Medical Assistance to Travelers, which is a non-profit organization dedicated to helping travelers who need medical assistance while abroad. Americans can write the association at 736 Center Street, Lewiston, NY 14092; Canadians can write it at 188 Nicklin Road, Guelph, Ontario NIH 7L5.

It is even a good idea to be prepared for travel in North America. For example, I like to vacation in the Canadian bush. If you enjoy similar activities, you ought to know something about being your own physician. You cannot count on there being any medical experts in the bush; or, putting it another way, there is no second aid. So first aid is not good enough to ensure survival. If you do not know how to perform a cricothyrotomy or suture a severe laceration or recognize and treat hypothermia, someone (including yourself) may die. And your enjoyment of the outdoors may be greatly decreased if you are unprepared to handle such medical problems as dental pain or outer ear infection or heat exhaustion or gingivitis. The book that I always take with me into the bush is *Wilderness Medicine* by William W. Forgey, M.D. If your internist believes that you know what you are about, he can provide you with the appropriate prescription drugs, tell you where to obtain the other supplies that you may need, and even teach you certain medical techniques such as the best way to suture a laceration. Incidentally, I have found Forgey's book very helpful around home: there's no point bothering your physician with a minor health problem if you know how to take care of it yourself. I recommend that every home have a copy of *The Columbia University College of Physicians and Surgeons Complete Home Medical Guide* (or some equivalent); it is extremely useful, interesting, and comprehensive.

The fifth step may be the most important of all: practice preventive medicine. This is the topic of the next three chapters. But good health habits are not enough.

Teach yourself to avoid being injured. Most injuries are due to carelessness, and carelessness can be avoided. I remember learning to use a band saw in shop class in junior high school: everyone, at first, was afraid of it. The trick, of course, was to stay afraid of it, to continue to respect its power to cut off your fingers. The ones who began to take it for granted were the ones who got cut. It's the same with riding a motorcycle or going into the bush or doing anything dangerous. Danger can always be minimized if carelessness is avoided. I recently learned about two men who fell off a scaffold that was several stories high; one spent months in the hospital with a broken back. Both men were experienced. But they were careless: not only weren't their safety harnesses tied to the scaffolding, the scaffolding itself was not even correctly fastened to the building! That accident would not have happened to beginners: beginners would have been so afraid that they would have checked everything three times. In the bush there's a saying: 'Always alert, never get hurt'. Treat home like the bush.

Our environment is beginning to harm us. We have so fouled the land and air and waters that our own pollution is beginning to threaten our survival. Yet we Americans not long ago elected a President who said that trees pollute! Our goal should be zero pollution. For example, the air and water that leave a factory should be as clean as the air and water that go into a factory. This is a problem throughout the world that will require concentrated political action to achieve lasting results. If we don't do it we may eventually die from it as surely as the trout in the Adirondack lakes.

3
Habits

Imagine yourself an objective observer studying for the first time the life of some human being or other. What would you observe? You would observe the behavior of that creature. And you would probably soon realize that nearly all of the behavior may easily be organized into types: sleeping or eating or driving or working or talking or loving and so on. You would not be able to observe directly such activities as thinking or choosing or hoping or wondering, but you would at least be able to observe some of the results (if any) of those activities. If you were able to observe all of these activities from the first person or internal point of view as well as from the third person or external point of view, you would learn that many of them are habitual.

Habitual activities, as Franklin suggests, should be evaluated as good, bad, or neutral. Habits are good if they increase the chances of your having a successful Project (your most important activity),[9] bad if they decrease the chances of your having a successful Project, and neutral if they have no effect upon it. (I am unable to think of a habit, however, that is entirely neutral.) Suppose, for example, that the Project that Alice has chosen to give meaning to her life is the Project of helping her fellow human beings to lower the rate of population growth. Her life's work, in other words, is to try to understand the causes of overpopulation and to educate others about how best to decrease the rate of growth. She learned that the world population in 1980 was about 4,000,000,000, which is about five times greater than it was in 1800 and about twelve times greater than it was in 1300. She realized that if we do not voluntarily control population growth, it will be involuntarily controlled by such traditional forces as famine, disease, and warfare. Believing that voluntary control is better than involuntary control, she chose the indicated Project. Her habits can be evaluated with respect to this major Project: her good habits will be those that increase the chances of her being successful and her bad habits will be those that decrease the chances of her being successful. For example, some of her physical habits are important with respect to her health and her health is important with respect to her chances of engaging in successful activities with respect to her Project. Should she become an alcoholic, her addiction to alcohol may interfere over the long run with her being successful. (She may even change her major Project to the Project of staying drunk, which is not a valuable one.) The same goes for addiction to tobacco or cocaine. Should she develop the habit of getting regular, comprehensive physical examinations, she increases her chances of being successful over the long run. The same for the develop-ment of good habits concerning diet and exercise.

In this Chapter I consider the elimination of bad health-related habits. In Chapters 4 and 5 I consider the develop-ment of good health-related habits.

Suppose that you actually have some physical habit that

you wish to eliminate. Perhaps, for example, your physician has told you to break your addiction to tobacco or alcohol or some other noxious substance. Rule number one is, of course, *Avoid making things worse.* But, we are supposing, you are in the habit of makings things worse. Let me use tobacco addiction, specifically smoking cigarettes, as an example. This is a good example because, according to the surgeon general, cigarette smoking is the number one preventable cause of death. Furthermore, I myself know something about it. At various times I have regularly smoked cigarettes (or a pipe and, occasionally, have smoked cigars and chewed tobacco). Since I have not done so for years, I am one of the millions of Americans who has broken the habit of smoking cigarettes. (In 1964 over 50 percent of white males in the U.S. smoked cigarettes; by 1984 that figure had dropped to 38 percent and the rate has continued to decline.) Furthermore, tobacco is a gateway drug; it opens the gates for the abuse of other drugs. But however good an example this is, it is only an example. My remarks are intended to apply to other bad habits with the appropriate modifications. Even a nonsmoker may find the following procedure interesting.

Consider an analogy. Suppose that you are a real estate investor and that an apartment house that you own has a leaky roof. In other words, you have a physical defect that you wish to remove. What should you do? There are several alternatives. i. You can do nothing. This amounts to deciding to let things get worse, to live with the problem, to let water damage the building. ii. You can decide to sell the building. This amounts to getting rid of the problem by passing it on to someone else. iii. You can decide to patch the roof. This temporary expedient amounts to deciding to postpone solving the problem. iv. Or you can decide to install a new roof. What should a wise investor do? A good decision in a certain case will depend upon the specific features of that case. But, in general, it would be unwise to decide to do nothing: the resulting water damage will only make the condition of the building deteriorate. Not only will you eventually have to do something about the leaky roof, but you may also have to fix rotted walls or an undermined foundation. It would also be unwise to sell the building just for this reason. If a buyer does not notice that the roof is leaky, you would be dishonest if you did not point it out. A wary buyer will notice it anyway. In either case, the buyer will simply deduct the cost of fixing the roof from the purchase price of the building. It might be expedient to patch the roof. Perhaps you do not have, and cannot raise, the money for a new roof. But it would be best to look at this defect as an opportunity to improve the condition of your building; it would be best if you decided to install a new roof. This solves the problem the right way and, should you sell the building, the price that you receive may actually more than offset the cost of the new roof. In general, a wise real estate investor will look at the defects of buildings as opportunities for improvement, will look for a way to turn a negative into a positive.

You, too, as we have imagined, have a physical problem, namely, the habit of smoking cigarettes. What are the alternatives? You could do nothing. This amounts to deciding to let things get worse, to live with the problem, to let your body further deteriorate. There is no longer any reasonable doubt about this. According to a recent statement by the American Medical Association, "smoking is associated with some 340,000 premature deaths a year, including 30 percent of all cancer deaths. Millions suffer from debilitating chronic disease caused by smoking. It is a major risk factor in cardiovascular disease, chronic bronchitis and emphysema, and cancer of the lung, throat, mouth, esophagus, pancreas, and bladder. It can also cause problems ranging from minor respiratory infections to stomach ulcers."[10] There is no way to pass on the bad habit or to patch it up, which are two points at which the analogy to the leaking roof breaks down. You could substitute a nicotine gum addiction for the tobacco addiction or you could decrease the number of cigarettes smoked daily. But neither of these alternatives stops all deterioration. Or you could quit smoking and break the bad habit. So the genuine alternatives are to do nothing or to quit.

But why bother to quit? After all, if quitting smoking were easy, all rational smokers would do it. Why should you deny yourself the pleasure of smoking? You may die tomorrow in an automobile accident; why not enjoy smoking until then? Living is difficult and smoking is one of your few pleasures, so why bother to quit? Besides, cigarettes are relatively inexpensive. Besides, smoking is a good way to handle stress. And it goes well with other important pleasures such as eating and drinking. So why quit? '

The chief reason has nothing at all to do with health or with pleasure: it has to do with being out of control. A cigarette smoker is a slave to tobacco. A smoker is not someone who is free to choose; a smoker *must* choose to smoke. Slavery is an evil. It is better to be free from the slavery of tobacco addiction than to be a slave to it. Isn't it better to control your own life than to let a plant control it? Who could disagree with the obvious answer?

Of course, you may pretend to yourself that you are free

not to smoke. But if this freedom not to smoke is never exercised, what evidence is there for it? We human beings have a great capacity for rationalizing, for creating conceptual illusions that screen us from reality. But living life behind a veil of illusions is not living life well. If we cannot be honest with ourselves, if we cannot tell the truth to ourselves, with whom can we be honest? How can we possibly live wisely, how can we possibly make consistently good decisions, if we live in a realm of unreality? Honest smokers admit to themselves that they are slaves to tobacco, and they often have a lowered self esteem because of that assessment. They would think better of themselves if they were able to become free from the addiction to tobacco. Many want to quit but have been unable to quit. Being an honest slave is at least better than being a dishonest slave.

The first step in solving a problem is recognizing the reality of the problem. Often, this first step is the most difficult. This is notoriously true of alcoholics: perhaps everyone who knows Billy knows that Billy is a drunk—except Billy! Whatever the habit, no bad habit can be overcome (except accidentally) without the recognition that it is a bad habit. (A smoking habit might be overcome accidentally, for example, if a smoker became permanently stranded without tobacco on a desert island.) But how does one recognize reality?

It is difficult. There is here no simple solution. There is no infallible guide to reality. There is no agreed-upon criterion of truth. Our powers of self-deception are too great. The briefest acquaintance with intellectual history demonstrates this, and probably the clearest sequence of episodes of intellectual history in which this becomes apparent is the shift from the medieval to the modern world. There was no generally recognized problem concerning the criterion of truth in the medieval world. For example, a typical illiterate European in the tenth century took it for granted that important truths were known by the ecclesiastical authorities; in other words, the pope or his minions could decide any relevant question. But did not different popes at different times declare different and sometimes inconsistent propositions to be true? And, anyway, how did a pope know the difference between a true proposition and a false one? Luther argued that a (religious) proposition can be known to be true only if it is what conscience is compelled to believe on reading the *Bible*. But do not different readers sometimes honestly interpret the *Bible* in different ways? How can we know that we have interpreted God correctly? Bacon argued that a proposition can be known to be true only if it is supported by sensory evidence. But, as skeptical philosophers were quick to point out, this ignores the phenomenon of perceptual variation: two perceivers may perceive the 'same' object differently (for example, I may see the apple as red and my colorblind father may not see it as red) or one perceiver may perceive the 'same' object differently at different times (for example, I may taste this apple as being sweet now but, if I don't now finish eating it and catch a cold in the meantime, it may taste bland tomorrow). How am I ever able to know that I am perceiving the world correctly? Galileo tried to answer this question by claiming that a proposition that is supported by sensory evidence can be known to be true only if the phenomenon in question exhibits a mathematical regularity. This entails two worlds: a 'real' objective world that can be measured, in other words, a world of shapes and sizes and motions, and an 'unreal' subjective world that

31

cannot be measured, in other words, a world of colors and tastes and feelings. But isn't, for example, the color of an apple just as real as its shape? The philosophical discussion concerning the criterion of truth, concerning the problem of how to recognize reality, has continued until the present day.

There is no easy way to recognize reality. Nobody has a special access to the truth. Of course, many people claim to have such access. There are two groups of people in particular who stand out: priests and scientists. Every priest claims to know the truth. Perhaps some priest does—but how do you and I recognize which one? Imagine ten priests from ten different religions in one room. Can you also imagine them agreeing about the truth of any religious proposition? Even if the beliefs of some given priest are internally consistent, they will be inconsistent with the beliefs of any priest of a different religion. How are we to know which dogma (if any) is correct? It is obviously stupid to accept some dogma sim-ply because our parents did. Parents are not necessarily religious authorities. Are there any religious authorities? If so, who are the religious authorities? Here, as elsewhere, the proper procedure is to evaluate the relevant evidence. A Christian priest, for example, might argue as follows: i. Only God could conquer death; ii. Jesus conquered death; iii. Nobody else has ever conquered death; (hence) Jesus and only Jesus is God. Is this a sound argument? The reasoning is good; the argument is valid. But are the premises true? It takes a good deal of work to determine a defensible answer here. And doing the work amounts to making yourself an authority on the Christian religion. If you choose to do this sort of work for every religion, then you are choosing to make yourself a religious authority. There is no rational alternative for determining which religious dogma, if any, is correct.[11] We should learn and consider and discuss the relevant ideas and then make the best judgments that we are able to make.

It is the same with scientists. They often pretend to have a special method for determining the truth: the so-called 'scientific' method. But, in fact, there is no such method; there is no method that is appropriate to all the generally-recognized sciences.[12] In fact, scientific experts are notorious for disagreeing among themselves. Imagine, for example, some carefully controlled, double-blind, randomized experiment to test a new drug. Give the results of the study to ten physicians and ask them to draw the correct conclusions. Can you imagine them all agreeing about the truth of any specific interpretation of the data? Perhaps one of the interpretations is correct—but how do you and I recognize which one? Or think of two psychiatrists on opposite sides in a courtroom. Priests and scientists are in the same boat that we are; we all share the human condition. They too must make their best interpretations and live with them. If so, develop a healthy skepticism concerning the beliefs of anyone who claims to be an expert. When a decision is important, the wisest course may be to educate yourself.

Knowledge is a good. It is better to know than to be ignorant. If so, it follows that self-knowledge is a good. The better I understand myself the more likely I am to make better decisions concerning my life. Persons who are wise will structure their habits on the basis of self-knowledge. But there is no special way to self-knowledge. Understanding in this area is like understanding in other areas. How do I come to understand something new? I relate the new object to objects that I have already understood; I relate it by noting the relevant similarities and differences.[13] This requires judgment. Each of us is unique. So the content of my self-knowledge will not be the same as the content of your self-knowledge—and this is always true for any two people.

Each of us is in a better position to understand ourself than someone else. But it is exactly this intimacy that causes us to lose perspective. This is one reason why having friends or relatives is valuable: they have a perspective on our lives that we ourselves lack. They often understand truths about us that we find difficult to grasp. Good, honest discussions with such people are often valuable. And it is the same in, for example, science or philosophy: good, honest discussions are often valuable and, indeed, their value is generally recognized. If, for example, Carol is a researcher who thinks that she has discovered a new drug that is effective in treating certain diseases, she marshals her evidence and publishes her results. Other researchers may test the new drug for themselves and argue either that her thesis is a good one or that it is not a good one. This sort of procedure is, in effect, a good, honest discussion. Philosophers, too, engage in such free, unrestricted, rational inquiry. It is, presumably, the reason why Plato wrote dialogues instead of monologues: he was discussing his ideas—not simply announcing them. In general, the clash of ideas is the greatest stimulator of intellectual progress. So a good way to develop your understanding in any area is to engage in good, honest discussion about it.

It may seem as if I have digressed far from the topic of quitting smoking. But I have not: self-knowledge here is important. But there are two difficulties: it is difficult to determine the truth about yourself, and what is true about you may not be true about another. Hence, a method of quitting that works for you may not work for another.

It is important to understand why the bad physical habit originated. Why, you must ask yourself, did you begin to smoke? The answer is likely to be 'peer pressure'. Cast your mind back to your first cigarette. What were you really trying to do? Were you trying to become one of the group? Or were you trying to imitate a respected older sibling or parent? Or were you thinking of yourself, for example, as glamorous as some idolized movie star? Or were you trying to do something else? Here is an opportunity to learn about yourself. What really motivated you? Why did you begin to smoke? Almost nobody starts smoking after the age of twenty-one; smoking almost always starts in youth. Didn't it in your case? Perhaps, like other youths, you needed to fit into a certain peer group and its pressure is what caused you to start. If that is your interpretation, ask yourself, 'How do I know that this is the correct interpretation?' It isn't an easy question to answer. Keep thinking about it.

How did smoking cigarettes become a habit? Didn't you cough when the smoke first hit your lungs? Didn't you have to teach yourself not to cough? Or was it pleasurable from the first drag? Answers here vary. Didn't you teach yourself to use tobacco to handle the stress of growing up? Didn't you teach yourself to enjoy smoking during study or work breaks or after eating or while drinking? Ask yourself honestly, now that you are an adult, do you still need the group acceptance you once did? Do you still need tobacco to handle stress? Do you still need tobacco to enjoy a glass of beer or a cup of coffee? Isn't your smoking habit really a juvenile habit?

Cigarette smokers are not fully in charge of their own lives.

They fully deserve their lowered self-esteem. (I am here assuming that a smoker's genetic make-up is irrelevant. Such an assumption is not warranted in the case of certain other addictions. For example, it is now common to distinguish two different types of alcoholics and the difference between them is thought to be caused by differences in genetic make-up; in other words, some alcoholics have more of a genetic predisposition to become alcoholics than other alcoholics. Obviously, those with a genetic predisposition may be praiseworthy for making valiant, even though unsuccessful, attempts to overcome their alcoholism. Similarly, some persons seem to have a genetic predisposition to become addicted to cocaine. A genetic predisposition in favor of addiction cannot lead to addiction unless the relevant substance is ingested. Anyone ignorant of their genetic predispositions would do well to avoid such substances as alcohol and cocaine in the first place. The same may be true for nicotine. But the error to be avoided is blaming your genes for your bad habits in cases in which the genes are not to blame.)

From the standpoint of health it is better never to have smoked than to have smoked and quit. But that is not necessarily true from a psychological standpoint. It is not easy to grow up in our uncertain world. If you have survived your adolescence with nothing worse than a cigarette habit, you have probably done a good job growing up. And learning to overcome that habit can put you ahead of someone who has never smoked with respect to self knowledge. In this sense, the negative can be turned into a positive. It should not be simply a matter of feeling guilty about smoking. It is a matter of facing the facts. Determine honestly why you started smoking and why you continued the habit. Ask yourself honestly if you wouldn't be better off as a nonsmoker. If the answer is 'yes,' then decide to quit. It is that simple.

Commit yourself to becoming a nonsmoker. This is, for the moment, only an intellectual commitment. But think about it carefully. Imagine, in detail, yourself as a non-smoker. You would no longer have to carry cigarette packages around with you—or lighters or matches. You would no longer have to go to the store on evenings when you run out of cigarettes. You would no longer have the expense of buying cigarettes or the expense of repairing burned dresses or suits or carpets. You will probably feel much better once you become a nonsmoker: you will probably sleep better and lose that hacking cough. You will certainly have the satisfaction of knowing that you are no longer actively undermining your health by smoking. Furthermore, you will look better: your fingers will lose their yellow stain and your teeth will be cleaner, too. You will begin to smell the world again—to smell the grass and the trees and the flowers. Your food will taste much better; you will enjoy it so much that you will have to watch that you don't gain too much weight. You will feel better about yourself for finding a more mature way to deal with stress, such as going for a brisk walk instead of smoking. You will actually feel more relaxed about yourself, more poised, more confident—once you have been a non-smoker for a couple of weeks. Your self-esteem will rise because you will know that you are no longer a slave to tobacco. Nonsmokers will no longer be offended by the smell of your hair or clothes or breath, and you will no longer be polluting the air that they breathe. People who learn that you are an ex-smoker will admire you for quitting. Wouldn't the quality of your life improve if you changed from a smoker to nonsmoker?

If so, you are well on your way. You have not only recognized the problem, you have begun to develop a determination to solve it. This is an example of treating a defect as an opportunity, an example of how to shift from a losing to a winning attitude. Of course, it is one thing to shift your attitude and another to quit smoking.

A necessary condition of quitting smoking is believing that it is possible for you to quit smoking. Someone who believes (like a Freudian) that your decisions are beyond your rational control believes that humans are not free. But such beliefs are false. The truth is that, in large measure, we are what we choose to be. We are not merely passive observers riding the causal train that comes from our heredity and environment. The qualification 'in large measure' is needed to cover cases such as quadriplegia: a quadriplegic need not choose to be a quadriplegic—a quadriplegic simply finds himself a quadriplegic. But being a smoker is not like being a quadriplegic. You chose to be a smoker; you made yourself into a smoker. And you are able to make yourself a nonsmoker again.

You became a smoker for certain reasons. You have been thinking about those reasons. They are less important than the reasons that you have decided not to smoke. You have already thought of certain reasons that will motivate you to quit being a smoker. They may be health-related or they may have to do with taking more control of your life. Determine for yourself exactly what they are. Then write them down. Take a 3" by 5" card and on it write your reasons for wanting to quit smoking. Do it now. Do not con yourself into thinking that you will always be able to remember them clearly: you are an addict and, when the urge to smoke strikes, you will not be thinking clearly about anything but smoking. Write down your reasons and keep that card within reach at all times—in your wallet or purse or near your bed. Soon, instead of pulling a cigarette out, you'll be able to pull your card out. That card, as strange as it may seem, will help you survive the urge to smoke without smoking.

Your habit of smoking cigarettes began voluntarily: you decided to try smoking and you continued to smoke. As you continued to decide to smoke the amount of attention that you paid to smoking diminished. You did not decide to become a smoker and from that moment onward you were a habitual smoker. You decided the first time to smoke for whatever reasons you had. Then you decided the second time, and the third time, and the fourth time, and so on. You began to associate smoking with being one of the group, with relieving stress, or whatever. You made your associations and your decisions and, when they had been made time after time after time, you paid less and less attention to them. Smoking became habitual. Now it is time to reverse the process.

Your smoking habit began voluntarily and can be stopped voluntarily. You have tentatively decided not to smoke. That is a voluntary decision. Observe yourself in action: observe yourself buying and carrying and taking out and lighting and inhaling and discarding cigarettes. Isn't it, really, a rather stupid and silly set of actions? Who in their right mind would ever have thought of it on their own? Does each cigarette really give you pleasure? Or do you just habitually smoke many of them without paying much attention at all to what you are doing? Does each cigarette really relieve stress? How many times a day do you really feel heavily stressed? Once?

Five times? And yet how many times a day do you smoke? Twenty times? Forty times? Do you always smoke only to relieve stress? If you smoke only one or two cigarettes a year, say when you learn of the death of a relative or friend or become otherwise heavily stressed, you are not a habitual cigarette smoker and there is no habit for you to break. But if you smoke five or twenty or fifty cigarettes a day, everyday, then you have developed a bad habit. It is ripe to be broken—because you have realized it.

There is no one method of quitting smoking that works for everyone. That's the bad news. But the good news is that, if so, this means that you have the opportunity of coming to understand more about yourself by finding, among the various methods, the one that works for you. The task is to find a method that works and to quit smoking.

For example, the method that worked for me is the one that Herbert Brean developed from the famous chapter on habit in William James's great work, *The Principles of Psychology*. You have already gone through the preliminaries. You have started thinking about quitting smoking. You have listed the reasons why you smoke. You have decided to try to quit because you are not afraid; you realize that, if one method does not work, you will simply find one that does. If you are afraid to try something, you will never succeed. And it is not failure that is so terrible; it is not trying. (Anyone who is wise thinks of failures as opportunities for learning.) You have been watching yourself as a smoker and waiting for a good time to become a nonsmoker again. You have been telling yourself that you will become a nonsmoker again, that it is just a matter of time. You are deliberately conning yourself; keep doing it because it works.

It is the positive side of our ability to rationalize; more about this later.

The method that I recommend is based on four principles. Try it for yourself. If it works, terrific. If not, find another method that works.

Pick a good time to quit—perhaps the start of a vacation or a birthday or New Year's. This is important because you want to *launch yourself on your new way of life with as much momentum as possible.* Give your resolution to quit every assistance. As James says, "[a]ccumulate all the possible circumstances which shall re-enforce the right motives; put yourself assiduously in conditions that encourage the new way; make engagements incompatible with the old . . . "[14] It may help you to take a public pledge. It may help to bet something that you really don't want to lose. Build up your momentum with every trick that you are able to think of. Once you have picked a good time and begun to develop momentum you are well on your way.

Forget about the idea of tapering off. (This does not apply to breaking all addictions.) When the good time arrives, quit. Never feed your addiction. *Make no exceptions.* As James says, "Never suffer an exception to occur till the new habit is securely rooted in your life . . . Continuity of training is the great means of making the nervous system act infallibly right".[15] Giving in even once will make it all the harder to quit. Never, not even once, light a cigarette or take a drag of a cigarette. It is simply astounding how quickly artificial desires die if they are never fed. You may have been smoking for decades, but your desire for tobacco will almost completely die out within two weeks—or less! So when the urge to smoke strikes, do not feed it. Read your card. Go for a walk. Chew gum. Do anything else but smoke a cigarette. The urge to smoke will rather quickly pass—and you will have reinforced your new procedure for handling it.

Initial success is crucial. If you fail at first, your enthusiasm for quitting will diminish. But if you succeed at first, your success will tend to breed more success. This is why it is so important to pick an auspicious moment to quit.

Becoming a nonsmoker, like becoming a smoker, does not involve one decision; it involves a whole series of decisions. We human beings are temporal creatures; our lives occupy a span of time. It is obvious that we cannot live different times at a single time. If the urge to smoke strikes and I decide not to smoke, that in itself does not make me a nonsmoker. I must decide again, the next time the urge to smoke strikes, to become a nonsmoker. And the time after that. Eventually, I will give less and less attention to this sort of decision; eventually, nonsmoking will become habitual. This conception has two consequences.

First, when the urge to smoke strikes, think only about this particular urge to smoke. This urge is the enemy—forget about the rest of your life. Your future is free from your present. Whether you smoke or not in the future depends upon what you decide to do in the future; it does not depend upon what you do now, in the present. So, *concentrate your efforts on the present* and forget about the future. Your enemy is this individual temptation; this is now the only important temptation. Forget about future ones.

Just as your future is free from your present, so your present is free from your past. Because you were a smoker in the past, you need not be a smoker in the present. Your decision to smoke last year does not determine whether or not you will smoke today. And if you falter and give in once to the urge to smoke, wipe that minor failure from your mind! You have made it harder on yourself by letting an exception occur, but that does not mean that you must fail. The fact that you smoked before does not mean that you must smoke now.

Second, *becoming a nonsmoker is a positive activity,* not a negative one. As James says, "Keep the faculty of effort alive in you by a little gratuitous exercise every day."[16] Instead of thinking of withdrawal symptoms, if any, as purely negative, try to think of them more positively as necessary encumbrances on the path of a higher good. They are, after all, marks of success: those who remain addicted never have any withdrawal symptoms and you, since you are breaking your addiction, are superior to those other addicts. What should you do if you want to become a nonsmoker and there is no particular urge to smoke to fight? Invent one. Go to your tobacconist and buy a pack of your favorite cigarettes. Open the pack and tamp them lovingly—as you used to. Smell the fragrant tobacco. Then crush the pack in your hand and throw it away. In other words, deliberately invent ways to expose yourself to tobacco. Deliberately practice being a nonsmoker, deliberately practice deciding not to smoke. The more you practice becoming a nonsmoker the more habitual it will become. The more habitual it becomes the freer you will be from tobacco addiction.

Just as human beings have the power for bad rationalizations, they have the power for good rationalizations. Recognition of this fact can make all the difference when you are engaged in the project of becoming a nonsmoker. For example, tell yourself that you want to be a nonsmoker because tobacco tastes horrible. (Didn't it taste horrible when you first tried it?) Even if you believe that it tastes good, tell yourself

43

frequently enough that it tastes horrible and you may eventually convince yourself! Each night as you go to sleep tell yourself that, whatever else you do the next day, you are not going to smoke. Convince yourself that tomorrow you are not going to smoke. You are too mature, now, to be a slave to tobacco. Besides, tobacco tastes horrible! This may sound too ridiculous to work, but I assure you that it does work.

Finally, learn to laugh at yourself. Isn't this situation that you've gotten yourself into absurd? Think of curing dried leaves off a bush, shredding and blending them, rolling them into a piece of thin paper, lighting one end, and sucking the resulting smoke into your lungs. The whole sequence is preposterous. Yet you cannot even watch a movie from beginning to end without doing it! Wow! So take your transformation as a serious project but don't lose your perspective entirely. Use your sense of perspective and your sense of humor to help you in your fight.

In summary, then, the four principles are these:
1. Launch yourself on your new way of life with as much momentum as possible.
2. Make no exceptions.
3. Concentrate your efforts on the present.
4. Make your reformation into a positive activity.

There are other aids as well. Your physician may have some ideas. Perhaps you should try nicotine gum to get you over the hump. Perhaps you should join a group. Whatever it takes, quit smoking—don't just take it out in good intentions. You'll feel better about yourself; the quality of your life will improve. You will live life more excellently; in other words, you will become wiser. And that is what this book is all about.

4

Food and Drink

We are what we eat. As the German pun has it, *man ist was man isst*, one is what one eats. If so, living well has something to do with eating well. Our general concern is with trying to answer the question, 'What sorts of decisions should we make in order to have the best chances of living well?' If we are to live as well as we are able to, what sorts of decisions concerning food should we make? What should we eat? And what should we drink?

Life devours itself. Except for green plants, organisms kill or use other organisms to sustain their lives. If we are to live, we must, either, kill (or, of course, have killed) other animals or plants and eat them or, at least, consume the products of other organisms (for example, milk, eggs, and apples). Assuming, controversially, that other kinds of animals have no rights, except for not eating other humans and for not wasting what we kill, there may be no good *moral* argument for restricting the kinds of organisms that we eat or the products of other organisms that we eat. But within these very broad limits, how should we choose what to eat?

Plato briefly considers this issue in his dialogue *Gorgias*. He argues that what is pleasant or pleasurable is not necessarily what is good. For example, a good man, say someone who is wise and brave, is obviously different from a bad man, say someone who is a fool and a coward. Yet the good man and the bad man feel pleasure and pain equally. If the good were identified with the pleasurable and the bad were identified with the painful, then the absurd conclusion would follow that "the evil man becomes just as bad and good as the good man, or even more good"[17]

If an argument for Plato's conclusion is sound, then we ought to avoid thinking that what is good is necessarily what is pleasurable and that what is bad is necessarily what is painful. I would put it this way: even though it is true that pleasure is a good, it is not true that pleasure is the only good—or even the most important good. Pleasure should be distinguished from its cause or causes and from its consequences, if any; pleasure is intrinsically valuable but certain pleasures may have evil causes or evil consequences. If so, we ought not necessarily to do what is pleasurable, although the pleasure that we derive from an activity is certainly one reason in favor of engaging in it. Just because someone enjoys sawing down trees or killing buffalo or raping women, the pleasure that is derived from any of these activities is not, by itself, a sufficient reason for engaging in them.

It seems, then, that there are good or excellent activities, that there are pleasures, and that what is pleasurable may differ from what is good. What, Plato asks, does this have to do with living our lives? We should distinguish an end (goal) from the means used to obtain it. Both pleasure and what is good may be considered as different ends. Plato calls activities that seek pleasure without regard for what is good "flatteries". He suggests that flatteries should be avoided because they are useless in obtaining what is good. For example, a politician who merely flatters a crowd isn't doing anyone any good. He may speak at random, play off the crowd, and whip both himself and the crowd into a pleasurable frenzy. Hitler, in fact, often did just that. By way of contrast,

> the good man who speaks for the best surely will not say what he says at random but with some purpose in view, just as all other craftsmen do not choose and apply materials to their work at random, but with the view that each of their productions should have a certain form. Look, for example, if you will, at painters, builders, shipwrights, and all other craftsmen—any of them you choose—and see how each one disposes each element he contributes in a fixed order, and compels one to fit and harmonize with the other until he has combined the whole into something well ordered and regulated. Other craftsmen in general and those we were speaking of just now, who have to do with the body, physical trainers and doctors, give order, I think, and discipline to the body.[18]

An excellent body is an ordered, disciplined body. Eating, as Plato makes clear in what follows, is a means to the excellence of the body. If you value what is good for your body, you will not eat randomly. You will eat what the re-levant experts such as physicians say you should eat.

But, you may object to Plato's thinking here, shouldn't eating, at least sometimes, be considered solely as an end in itself? Why isn't the hedonist correct when he simply identifies what is good with what is pleasurable? Suppose, for example, that some Platonist argues that you ought not to eat chocolate cake for dessert this evening because it would not be good for you to eat it. But, some hedonist might reply, it would be good for you to eat it because you would find it delicious (pleasurable to taste). Or, he might continue, even if it were true that you ought not to eat it, that would only be because you will live longer if you forgo this particular pleasure and that would be good solely because it would enable you to enjoy more pleasures.

Reflections such as these may be used to raise a host of interesting issues.[19] At the risk of appearing dogmatic or too theoretical, permit me to advance some relevant foundational ideas that are necessary to evaluate hedonism.

Reality is everything that exists. We are able to be aware of existents. Existents are whatever is recognizable.

Existents are divisible into those that are concrete and those that are abstract. Concrete existents (individuals, entities) are spatiotemporal objects such as rocks, lakes, and lions or such as actions (for example, my snapping my fingers), activities (for example, your reading this book), and events (for example, a tornado's destroying a town). Abstract existents (properties, 'universals') are features of concrete existents that they may or may not share. For example, since two shirts may both be red, redness is an abstract existent; since one rock may be larger than another rock, size is an abstract existent. So an ordinary thing such as a rock is a concrete existent that has ('instantiates', 'exemplifies') some abstract existents. This rock, for example, has size, color, shape, weight, texture, spatial location, temporal location and so on.

Assuming that goodness is an existent, is it a concrete existent or an abstract existent? Concrete existents are what are usually thought or said to be good; if so, goodness is not itself a concrete existent. For example, suppose that Nick severs an artery in an accident and that Susan, who happens to be a physician, staunches the bleeding and saves his life. What she did was good; her behavior had the property of being good. Is goodness, then, an abstract existent, a property?

Abstract existents are what are sometimes thought or said to be good. The hedonist, for example, thinks that pleasure is good. Or, to return to the previous example, the reason that what Susan did was good was because she knew what to do to save his life. In other words, her behavior was her use of her knowledge that had the consequence of preserving his life. In this sense, her knowledge was primarily what was good and, because of that, her administering first aid was derivatively what was good; similarly, his life was primarily what was good and, because of that, her saving it was derivatively what was good.

If so, two important consequences follow. First, 'good' has at least two different, though related, senses. In the primary sense, it is applicable to some abstract existents such as pleasure, knowledge, and life. Properties that directly exemplify goodness are *abstract goods*. In the secondary sense, it is applicable to some concrete existents such as Susan's behavior. Some concrete existents, then, directly exemplify properties that, in turn, directly exemplify goodness; in other words, some concrete existents indirectly exemplify goodness and, to the extent that they do, they are *concrete goods*. Second, goodness, though an abstract existent or property, is not just another abstract existent, not just a property among other properties. Goodness is a property *of* properties. To use an analogy, goodness is 'higher than' those properties that are *of* concrete existents. This may have been what Plato was suggesting in the well-known, but obscure, passage in *The Republic* in which he discusses the 'form' of the good. As "fair" as knowledge and truth are, "[s]till higher honor belongs to the possession and habit of the good".[20] Concrete existents indirectly 'participate in' the 'form' of the good (goodness) if they 'participate in' 'forms', which are abstract existents, that directly 'participate in' goodness itself. For example, since beauty is good, it is good for a concrete existent such as a work of art or a woman to be beautiful.

The best way to understand the difference between a concrete good and an abstract good is to distinguish, following Aristotle, between accidental predication and essential predication. Roughly, there is an important difference between the claim that Socrates is a man and the claim that Socrates is white: Socrates would not be what he is if he were not a man, but he could be what he is if he were not white. In other words, it is essential that Socrates be a man but it is not essential that he be white. He must exemplify the property of being a man but he need not exemplify the property of being white. More precisely, there is an analogy between, for example, 'being red is being colored' and 'being human is being an animal' in the sense that something cannot be red without being colored and something cannot be human without being an animal. These are cases of essential predication. The attribution of goodness to an abstract existent is a case of essential predication. To claim, for example, that pleasure is good is to claim that something cannot be pleasurable without being good. You can, as it were, know in advance that anything that has the property of being

50

pleasurable will automatically have the property of being good. The attribution of goodness to a concrete existent is a case of accidental predication. You cannot, as it were, know in advance which concrete existents will have the property of being pleasurable, and, so, which will indirectly have the property of being good. For example, before you had ever tasted one, could you have infallibly predicted whether or not the activity of drinking a glass of beer would be pleasurable? Of course not. In fact, if my experience here is typical, even after many beer-drinking experiences you cannot predict in advance: sometimes beer tastes delicious and sometimes it doesn't taste good at all.

If this argument is sound, goodness is an abstract existent—though a peculiar one. It is not merely one property among other properties; it is a principle for classifying other properties and, indirectly, for classifying concrete existents. Properties that are good are abstract goods; pleasure, beauty, and knowledge are examples.[21] Correspondingly, properties that are evil are abstract evils; pain, ugliness, and ignorance are examples. Various concrete existents exemplify abstract goods and abstract evils.

This provides the foundations of a theory for, among other things, evaluating hedonism. Hedonism is the claim that goodness is to be understood solely in terms of pleasure.

Permit me to restrict the use of 'pleasure' to the paradigmatic bodily pleasures. Pleasures are not all alike; they may be classified in different ways. For example, some ('lower') pleasures are spatial in the sense that they are experienced as having a location in space, for example, in the mouth or in the body as a whole, while some ('higher') pleasures are nonspatial. But the 'higher' pleasures are not, strictly speaking, pleasures at all; rather, they may be understood as our being conscious of the goodness of the relevant objects. For example, the pleasure of composing a sonnet is just our awareness that the activity of writing poetry is good; the pleasure of reading a great novel is just our awareness that the activity of reading great literature is good; the pleasure of solving a difficult equation is just our awareness that the activity of mathematical thinking is good.

Hedonism is plausible because it is true, as I have already admitted, that all pleasures (as distinct from their causes or consequences) are intrinsically good. Pleasure is an abstract good. Whatever has the property of being pleasurable has the property of being good.

But hedonism is implausible because it is false that pleasure is the only abstract good. Hedonists typically believe that only pleasure is what makes something valuable as an end, that pleasure is the criterion of intrinsic goodness.[22] Sometimes hedonists argue as follows: i. Only pleasure is desired as an end; ii. What is desired as an end, and only what is desired as an end, is good as an end; hence, iii. Only pleasure is good as an end. The idea that abstract goods are desirable because they are pleasurable is, as Aristotle and Butler argued, exactly backwards: we (often) find abstract goods (or, more strictly, concrete existents that exemplify abstract goods) pleasurable because we desire them and we desire them because they are good. For example, we enjoy knowing things because we understand that knowledge is good. Hedonism, then, like many ethical theories, is too simplistic.

Even if all this is correct, there is much more to be said about goodness and pleasure. Though I return to similar theoretical considerations in the last chapter, this is not the place for a general theory.

Returning to the topic of food, hunger is a paradigm of a bodily desire. The good with respect to hunger is the satisfaction of the hunger. Pleasure may or may not accompany the satisfaction of the hunger (which is similar to the fact that pleasure may or may not accompany drinking a glass of beer). Normally, eating is an activity that exemplifies gustatory pleasures. But, for example, if you lost your sense of taste you could still satisfy your hunger by eating even if that activity were not to exemplify any gustatory pleasures. The satisfaction of the hunger is the extinction of the hunger. (This is why it is senseless to claim that the state of being satisfied is pleasurable; since pleasure is something and extinction is nothing, extinction cannot be pleasurable.) So the good with respect to hunger is freedom from hunger. The Stoics, then, were right: the good with respect to (bodily) desire is peace, in other words, freedom from the desire.

A hungry person may eat any amount of food and still be hungry. (This was one of the tortures that Dante missed in the *Inferno*!) Hunger is the desire to eat; eating is the aim of hunger. But eating is not the good with respect to hunger: eating need not be good nor even thought of as good. Distinguish the aim of the desire from its satisfaction: eating is the aim of hunger, for example, even if eating does not result in satisfaction or even if eating were not expected to result in satisfaction. Again, the satisfaction of the desire is the freedom from the desire.

There is such a thing as the desire for pleasure itself. If food is pleasurable, we may continue eating even after we have ceased being hungry solely in order to continue to experience further gustatory pleasure. What this may be is nothing but the consciousness that possible future pleasures will be good.

Since pleasure is good, it is obviously good for a meal, an episode of eating food, to be pleasurable (and, indirectly, to be good). A meal is a concrete existent. Every concrete existent exemplifies more than one property. A rock has size and color and shape and so on. Similarly, meals are complex. Some of the foods eaten may be pleasurable to the palate and some may not. A single meal may exemplify different abstract goods. For example, assuming that conversation is part of the meal, a meal may exemplify friendship as well as pleasure. Or it might exemplify simultaneously both an abstract good and an abstract evil. This would be a bit like thinking of a single item of food, say a stew, as exemplifying both an abstract good (for example, if it were pleasurable because it tasted good) and an abstract evil (for example, if it were deadly because it was laced with a powerful poison that was itself tasteless and odorless). What is it that really counts about meals, about eating food?

Well, what is it about us that really counts when we engage in the activity of eating? It is not, for example, our ability to be friends; since eating can be done alone it is not essentially an activity that exemplifies the abstract good of friendship. It is not, for example, our ability to experience pleasure; I have just argued that eating is not essentially an activity that exemplifies the abstract good of pleasure. What is essential is that eating is one of the ways in which we are *like* other living animals. Mountains and machines, clouds and clumps of earth, do not eat; only living organisms eat, only things like polar bears and porpoises, smallmouth bass and starlings. The next logical question is: what is the good with respect to a living organism? It is universally recognized to be health. The abstract good that characterizes living things is the property of being healthy; the corresponding abstract evil would be being diseased. This is probably the underlying reason why Plato evaluated diet, all our meals, solely as a means to the end of health. That much a philosopher can do.

The next step is for scientists, specifically, nutritional experts. Which diets are healthful? First, how do nutritional experts determine which diets are healthful? The general answer is that experts determine which nutrients the healthy human body needs and they then figure out which foods (prepared in which ways) provide those nutrients. So the basic idea is quite simple. Determine which nutrients the body needs for good health. Determine which (available) foods have which nutrients. Determine how the nutritional value of food changes during preparation. And then simply match the list of the body's nutritional needs with the list of properly prepared foods.

But there are at least five complicating factors. First, the nutritional experts are still learning. Not everything about nutrition is yet known. Therefore, not surprisingly, experts differ on their general recommendations. They know that the human body needs certain amounts of certain vitamins, minerals, proteins, carbohydrates, fats, and fiber. But the experts do not agree completely on the kinds of nutrients needed in general.

Second, not only will the human body physically deteriorate if it does not get enough of the proper sorts of each of the needed nutrients, it will also physically deteriorate, by becoming obese, if it gets too much of otherwise beneficial nutrients.

There is no ideal amount of these nutrients that is applicable to everyone. For example, a lineman in the National Football League needs different quantities of certain nutrients than does a petite fashion model. Furthermore, the metabolisms of different persons may process foods differently. For example, two persons each ingesting an equal amount of milk may derive different nutritional value from it.

Third, there is no one perfect food. You must do more than merely determine for yourself your own optimum amount of one food. A plethora of foods is available in North America from which to choose. But each sort of food has a different nutritional value. For example, one medium-sized banana has different amounts of vitamins, carbohydrates, and so on than one medium-sized Granny Smith apple. And individual food items of the same sort often have different nutritional values. For example, a large banana has slightly different amounts of certain vitamins, carbohydrates, and so on than a small banana.

Fourth, different people have different tastes. This is significant because we tend to live in groups and therefore tend to obtain, prepare and eat foods together. It will do me no good if my wife prepares, say, a squash for dinner if I don't like it and won't eat it.

On the other hand, tastes can change. If you, for example, begin to drink skim milk instead of regular milk on the advice of your physician you may not like it at first. But after a while you may come to like it so much that a glass of regular milk will taste as if you were drinking cream. It is possible to educate your tastes—as anyone who has learned to appreciate fine wine or cheese can attest. This fact spawns hope for any of us wanting to improve our dietary habits. Suppose that

Jim is obese and finds it difficult to abstain from cookies and cakes and pies and ice cream and other sweet 'junk' food. And suppose that Jim survives his first heart attack and decides that it is finally time to do something about his sweet tooth. Jim quits sweets 'cold turkey'. And a funny thing happens: he rather quickly loses his taste for them. After a while, if he were to eat a large piece of chocolate cake, he would feel queasy.

This is rather like a smoker. Suppose that Kelly is a smoker who finds it difficult to abstain from cigarettes. And suppose that Kelly survives her first heart attack and decides that it is finally time to do something about her cigarette habit. Kelly quits smoking 'cold turkey.' And a funny thing happens: she rather quickly loses her taste for cigarettes. After a while, if she were to smoke a cigarette, she would feel queasy. Insofar as this is a good analogy, the techniques in Chapter 3 are applicable to getting rid of bad dietary habits.

A fifth complicating factor is that different cultures have different habits and taboos about eating. There is no known culture that lacks them. There are (or, at least, originally were) reasons for all these habits and taboos, but many of these reasons have lost their justification. Nevertheless, since they are part of what makes us human, they cannot be ignored. Put it this way: all animals eat. Human animals alone, however, dine. It is part of our superiority to the rest of the animal kingdom. For nutritionists, this is a complicating factor. For diners, it is an opportunity.

It is far beyond the scope of this chapter to define the various kinds of nutrients, to list the current general recommendations concerning the daily amount of each of the various kinds, to list the nutritional values of commonly available foods, and to specify the ways that different food preparation techniques change nutritional values. An excellent single source is Jane E. Brody's *Jane Brody's Good Food Book: Living the High-Carbohydrate Way*. Its first three parts (over 225 pages) contain the theoretical background—including a chapter on exercise. The fourth part is on proper food preparation and the fifth part contains wholesome recipes. There are other good sources of information available on all these matters. The Harvard and Berkeley medical newsletters recommended in the previous chapter are excellent sources, as is the FDA Consumer, and free reprints are available from the government's Pueblo, Colorado, outlet. I subscribe to, enjoy, and recommend the *Tufts University Diet and Nutrition Letter.* Part Two of Kenneth Cooper's *The Aerobics Program for Total Well-Being* is a sensible popular guide. Another is Nathan Pritikin's *The Pritikin Program for Diet and Exercise* ; it is too severe, but it is nevertheless useful. The best place to go for specific advice is to your physician. If you have the motivation and educational background and simply want to understand more about nutrition, he may recommend something like *Living Nutrition*, edited by Fredrick J. Stare and Margaret McWilliams, or *Nutrition: An Integrated Approach* edited by Ruth L. Pike and Myrtle L. Brown. If you require a special diet to lose weight or to reduce the amount of cholesterol or other fatty substances in your blood or to treat some other abnormality, he may recommend something like one of the booklets from the American Heart Association on planning fat-controlled meals.

I have four general suggestions for eating well:
1. Select a balanced variety of foods.
2. Prepare food properly.
3. Eat the proper amount of food.

4. Work to make your meals enjoyable.

1. *Select a balanced variety of foods.* Contrary to what some gluttons or gourmets may believe, your sole Project should not be eating well. However, eating well is part of the best sorts of lives for two reasons: it can itself be a pleasant activity and, more importantly, it can contribute to the success of your Project. Eating well contributes to the success of your Project by improving and maintaining the chances of your being in overall good health and by improving and maintaining your energy level. If you are in ill health, you will be successful only by overcoming the problems caused by ill health; if you are in good health, you will not have to overcome health problems to be successful. If you have little energy, you will be successful only by overcoming that lack of energy; if you have a high level of energy, you will be able to work hard without having to overcome listlessness. Maximum benefits can only be obtained by eating a balanced variety of foods.

Without a balanced variety of foods, without proper nutrition, the value of other positive physical habits will be decreased. In fact, without proper nutrition one may lack the energy to develop other positive habits, such as exercising regularly.

What is a properly balanced variety of foods? The answer lies in dividing your daily consumption of calories into several essential kinds to ensure that you obtain a certain amount of your daily caloric intake from each of the kinds. The number of kinds is not agreed upon. A simple but satisfactory way, however, is to divide calories into three major sources: complex carbohydrates, protein, and fat. The exact amount of your optimum daily caloric intake from each of these three kinds is unknown, but it is reasonably believed that there should be some intake from each of the three.

Experts also agree that too much caloric intake from certain of these kinds is detrimental. For example, it is currently estimated that the average American gets about 40 or 45 percent of his daily caloric intake from *fat*. Most authorities agree that this percentage is too high; they argue that it should be reduced to 30 percent or less. Fat should not be eliminated entirely, however, because it serves a variety of essential functions. It would be impractical to reduce your fat intake to less than 10 percent. An intake of 15 to 25 percent is reasonable and would doubtless be a great improvement over the current 40–45 percent intake. But why do we need fats at all? To answer, we need to know something about how fats function in nutrition.

Fats are essentially composed of fatty acids and glycerol. A fatty acid is a chain of carbon atoms, and each carbon atom has attached hydrogen atoms. When each carbon atom has as many hydrogen atoms attached to it as it can hold (two), it is a saturated fatty acid. When two neighboring carbon atoms are lacking a hydrogen atom and a double bond forms between them, it is a mono-unsaturated fatty acid. When there is more than one such double bond in the chain, it is a poly-unsaturated fatty acid. Whether a food fat is from an animal or plant source, it will contain a mixture of saturated and unsaturated fatty acids. Though fats of animal origin are generally more saturated than fats of plant origin, there is variation within each group. For example, coconut oil and chocolate are highly saturated even though they are fats of plant origin. Beef has a higher percentage of saturated fatty acid than fish even though both are of animal origin. These different kinds of fat are important because each kind has different dietary effects. For example, saturated fats tend to raise the level of blood cholesterol while polyunsaturated fats tend to lower that level. (High levels of cholesterol and other fatty substances in the blood are risk factors of such physical abnormalities as coronary atherosclerosis and coronary heart disease.)

Fats are important. They provide linoleic acid, carry fat-soluble vitamins and aid in their absorption, and are a concentrated source of energy. They also add flavor and improve the texture of foods. We have evolved the ability to store fat, but unfortunately too much deposited fat results in being overweight or obese, which is unhealthy. One additional point about fat: It is very easy to underestimate the total fat in your diet. There are many easily visible sources of fat in the average American's diet: think of butter, margarine, lard, cooking oil or spray, and salad oil. But there are many less visible sources of fat as well: think of the fat particles and streaks in meat from domestic animals, sausage, cold cuts, duck, goose, and poultry skin. And there are hidden sources of fat as well: think of frankfurters, fish roe, whole milk dairy products, commercial breads and bakery goods, commercial mixes for breads and bakery goods, desserts (pies, cakes, puddings, custards, cookies, ice creams, whipped cream desserts, and pastries), sauces and gravies, commercially fried foods such as potato chips, thick soups, chocolate, commercial popcorn, chocolate fudge, and non-dairy creamers. When all these ubiquitous foods are counted, it is not difficult to understand why the average American's fat intake is so high.

Good nutrition is a matter of balance. We ought to obtain some, but not too much, of our daily caloric intake from fat.

The same goes for the other major sources of calories: vitamins, minerals, proteins, carbohydrates and dietary fiber. All ought to be balanced. And, of course, these nutrients are already combined in various foods. For example, one cup of whole cow's milk (3.5 percent fat by weight) provides 150 calories. It is 47 percent fat, 23 percent protein, and 29 percent carbohydrate. It provides 9 grams of total fat; it provides 5 grams of saturated fatty acids, 3 grams of monounsaturated fatty acids, and a trace of polyunsaturated fatty acids. It provides 34 milligrams of cholesterol. It provides 8 grams of protein. It provides 11 grams of carbohydrates. And this is just one food: imagine the complexity of trying to obtain this sort of information for each food item and combining it into menus that will provide reasonably tasty meals!

Some simplification is needed. I suggest the following: the three crucial major food groups are the complex carbohydrates, protein, and fat. About 60 percent of our daily caloric intake should come from the carbohydrates, about 20 percent from protein, and about 20 percent from fat. This is just a rough guideline: it would be extremely difficult to stick to it exactly—even if it were known to be the best possible general guideline, which it is not. But I suggest it as a practical, reasonable guide.

There are three sorts of *carbohydrates*. The simplest sugars (monosaccharides) such as glucose and fructose are the building blocks of most common carbohydrates. The double sugars (disaccharides) such as sucrose and lactose contain two simple sugars. The complex carbohydrates (polysaccharides) such as starch unite many simple sugars. Simple carbohydrates (monosaccharides and disaccharides) require no digestion; when ingested, they simply flood the body and quickly disappear. They are concentrated foods that have almost no nutritional value (although they may satisfy a sweet tooth, a learned craving for them). They also have deleterious effects: they tend to make fat, raise the level of certain blood lipids (triglycerides), and stress the pancreas. Hence, simple carbohydrates such as cane or beet table sugar, molasses, syrup, and honey should be avoided.

By way of contrast, we metabolize the complex carbohydrates rather slowly; they provide a steady, slow supply of glucose. (Glucose is the brain's only food.) A diet rich in unrefined complex carbohydrates is a diet that is unlikely to lead to any blood sugar problems and, hence, a diet that is unlikely to lead to great swings in energy levels. Body cells burn carbohydrates more efficiently, more cleanly, than they burn either protein or fat. So a diet rich in mainly unrefined complex carbohydrates is less likely to lead to long-term abnormalities than a diet rich in either protein or fat. And such a diet is a natural diet.

The following are good sources of complex carbohydrates: the cereal grains (for example, wheat, rice, corn, and oats), potatoes, many sorts of vegetables, many sorts of fruits, fruit juice, beans, peas, lentils, pasta, and whole-grain bread. In general, the less such foods are processed the better.

The *protein* in food must be digested. During digestion, protein is broken down to amino acids and absorbed into the blood. In order for the amino acids to perform their crucial function of building and maintaining body tissues efficiently, they must be in a well-balanced mixture. The human body can make certain amino acids; they are therefore 'nonessential' in terms of their dietary origin. Other amino acids must be obtained by the body preformed in foods; they are therefore

63

'essential' in terms of their dietary origin. The body requires different amounts of the essential amino acids. Food proteins that provide all of the essential amino acids in the proportions needed by the human body are high quality or complete proteins; food proteins that lack or are low in one or more of the essential amino acids are of lower quality (limiting, incomplete). Human bodies more closely resemble other animal bodies than plants. Animal products contain a better variety and balance of amino acids than do plant foods. Meat, fish, poultry, game (for example, deer or moose), and dairy products such as milk, cheese, yogurt, and eggs are excellent sources of high quality protein. Plant foods usually have less protein in their tissues than do animal products and they are usually low in one or more of the essential amino acids. However, combinations of proteins from different plant foods can complement one another and provide improved total protein quality. Legumes (peas and beans) and nuts (even processed as in peanut butter) provide larger amounts and better quality protein than other plant foods.

Two further points about protein. First, the body's need for protein has often been exaggerated. When was the last time that you heard of someone suffering from protein deficiency? Even among children in backward countries the problem is not generally one of too little protein but of too few calories. Nevertheless, some persons such as world-class bodybuilders may have a slightly higher than average need for protein. In such exceptional cases, it would be reasonable to modify my overall suggestions about caloric intake; I would suggest 60 percent from complex carbohydrates, 30 percent from protein, and 10 percent from fat. Second, protein from plant food has an important advantage over protein from animal products: it is much less likely to contain undesirable levels of fats and cholesterol. For example, the egg yolk from one large chicken egg contains nearly what one day's entire intake of cholesterol should be.

To summarize, selecting a balanced variety of foods means selecting roughly the following percentages of your daily caloric intake: 60 percent from complex carbohydrates, 20 percent from protein, and 20 percent from fat. If you do this, and eat a variety of foods within each of these three major categories, it is likely that you will obtain all the essential nutrients from the other categories (for example, minerals, vitamins, and dietary fiber). Just as an added precaution, it does not hurt to take a multi-vitamin pill (or a multi-vitamin pill with extra vitamin C) daily—though it is a waste of money if one has selected a proper balance of foods.

2. *Prepare food properly.* It obviously makes little sense to select foods to obtain the right amount of certain nutrients and then to change those amounts drastically while preparing the foods for eating. For example, it would be silly to select a potato because it is high in complex carbohydrates and low in fat and then to prepare it by deep frying it in animal fat. Or it would be silly to eat a serving of peas after boiling them in water, because part of their nutritional value would be lost to the water, which is usually discarded. If anything, we should try to improve the nutritional value of foods during preparation. For example, it is a good idea to remove the skin from poultry before eating the poultry. We should prepare food properly.

One obvious plan is to select recipes from sources whose authors demonstrate good nutritional judgment. I've already mentioned *Jane Brody's Good Food Book*. There is also *The*

Pritikin Program for Diet and Exercise by Nathan Pritikin and Patrick M. McGrady, Jr., which contains a number of excellent recipes, as does *Heart Smart: A Plan for Low-Cholesterol Living* by Gail L. Becker, R.D. Such books are much more plentiful than they were ten or twenty years ago. Of course, your physician, if he knows anything about cooking, may be a source of excellent advice.

Here are some general examples of proper food preparation. *a.* In general, the best ways to cook foods so that they retain their maximum nutritional value are to microwave, bake, or steam them. *b.* Use a rack when broiling, roasting, or baking foods. This permits the fat to drain off. And do not defeat the purpose of the rack by basting the food from the fatty fluid that accumulates in the bottom of the pan; keep the food moist by pouring a fresh fluid (for example, wine, tomato juice, or bouillon) over it. *c.* Prepare foods that cook in a liquid (for example, stew) a day ahead of time. After storing them in the refrigerator overnight, remove the hardened fat from the top and reheat before serving. Do the same for gravies and sauces. *d.* When possible, avoid pan-frying or deep-fat frying. Meats should be browned under the broiler rather than in a frying pan. *e.* Avoid preparing any packaged or prepared foods that contain fat—for example, regular cake mixes, regular frozen dinners, and vegetables frozen in butter sauce. *f.* Teach yourself how to bake breads. Not only will you be able to control the ingredients, the bread that you bake at home will be more likely to please your palate and nostrils than commercially baked bread. I strongly recommend Brody's chapter on breads and rolls;[23] I also recommend James Beard's *Beard On Bread* although you would be wise to limit the amount of salt and fat in his recipes.

3. *Eat the right amount of food.* Persons who are voluntarily underweight require immediate medical and psychological care. This is true whether the form of malnutrition is something as well-publicized as anorexia nervosa or something as little known as nutritional arrhythmia. If any form of malnutrition is suspected, consult your physician. I discuss in this section only persons who are voluntarily overweight. Many more North Americans suffer from being overweight than from being underweight.

Obesity is the state of being too fat. Obviously, then, it comes in degrees. The more obese you are the more unhealthy you are likely to be. If you had to choose between being fifteen and fifty pounds overweight, it would be better to be the former than the latter. But you do not have to choose between such alternatives: you can choose not to be overweight at all. It may be that *any* extra fat can be a catalyst for serious health problems; the medical experts are still learning about obesity.

What they have already learned is alarming enough. Obesity can be fatal. It is certainly uncomfortable. And it can cause or aggravate a number of serious health problems including hypertension (high blood pressure), coronary heart disease, gallbladder disease, liver disease, osteoarthritis, the emergence of latent diabetes, varicose veins, and a host of other health problems that can shorten life or detract from its quality.

How can you tell if you are obese? It is not always easy. *i.* Try standing naked in front of a full-length mirror and looking at yourself. Is there a roll of fat around your middle? Is there any 'dead' flesh on the back of your thighs? When you move an arm horizontally, does the fat swing freely on the lower side of your upper arm? The problem with this technique is that we get so accustomed to looking at fat people (including ourselves) that they look normal. I teach college and half my students are already fat! It constantly amazes me as I walk across campus: half the world seems to be waddling along. *ii.* Ask your physician if you are fat. He may be able to tell just by looking at you. *iii.* There are certain crude measurements of the percentage of body fat that can be taken easily in the physician's office. For example, he may do a skinfold examination by using a caliperlike instrument to pinch the outside fat. *iv.* The best way to determine the percentage of body fat is quite involved and expensive. It involves underwater measurements to determine specific gravity, total body volumetric determinations, and ultrasonic measurement of fat thickness. But these are not usually necessary. If you cannot tell by simply looking, try going swimming. If you are able to sink like a stone, you are probably not obese; if you are able to float quite easily, you are probably obese. The chief cause of obesity is over-consumption of calories: we simply consume more calories, more energy, than we expend. Persons who do not eat more than they need to do not get fat. Have you ever heard of an obese person emerging from a concentration camp after a year or two of incarceration? It is true that some obesity is caused by endocrine gland disorders—but the 'some' refers to only 1 or 2 percent of all obese persons. Obesity does not seem to be a matter of heredity; it seems to be a matter of environment. Of course, modern food processing, packaging, and advertising have contributed to the problem; it is so easy and convenient to shop for food and to eat out that many people simply tend to overindulge.

If you become obese by consuming more calories than you expend, you will become less obese by either consuming fewer calories than you need or by expending more calories or both. I consider how best to expend more calories in the next chapter. Physical exertion is important with respect to obesity for two reasons. (Have you ever seen a fat professional basketball or soccer player?) *i.* Calories that are consumed and are not used for physical exertion are converted into fat storage deposits in the body. *ii.* With only low levels of physical exertion, the normal 'internal' mechanisms that regulate appetite and the feeling of satiety do not operate properly. A fat, inactive person may be able to eat an enormous quantity of food before feeling full. This is an example of how the body adjusts to being fat. One problem for an obese person is to get the body to adjust again to being of the correct weight. This is not just a matter of how one feels. (An adult male who quickly loses twenty pounds may not feel as good at the lighter weight because his familiar and comforting heft may be missing.) It is also a matter of the body's metabolism: the metabolism of a fat person who suddenly consumes fewer calories each day may actually slow down. It is as if the body is protecting itself from starvation.

So it is not a good idea to rely on how you feel—because how you feel may be abnormal. Upon what should you rely?

The usual answer is: calories. The idea is quite sensible: determine your total daily caloric need and do not consume more than that number of calories. For example, suppose that Lenny is an obese, thirty-year-old male, and his physician recommends that he go on a 1,500 calory a day reducing diet until he reaches his proper weight, and a 2,200 calory a day maintenance diet thereafter. But sensible is not practical. In order for Lenny to follow his physician's advice, he must not only know the caloric value of everything that he eats and drinks, but he must also weigh or measure each portion of everything that he eats and drinks and keep a running total throughout the day. This is simply too much bother. Even if Lenny does it for a few months, it is unlikely that he'll do it forever. Or put it this way: going *on* a reducing diet implies that there will be a time when one goes *off* a reducing diet.

The goal is not simply to lose weight; the goal is to lose weight permanently (in other words, for five years and beyond). The only way to do that is to make permanent changes in your eating habits. And the best way to do that is to begin to get regular, moderate exercise in addition to beginning to change your eating habits. If you merely reduce your caloric intake, the weight that you lose will probably be about equally divided between muscle tissue and fat tissue. But if you reduce your caloric intake and exercise properly, the weight that you lose will probably be almost entirely fat.

But how do you make permanent changes in your eating habits? It is not easy. That is the bad news. And that is why it usually takes some traumatic physical experience such as a heart attack to motivate people to change. But it is possible. That is the good news. I myself have done it. I struggle with obesity every day. But my weight is now around 190—instead of around 230 where it was fifteen years ago.[24] I have permanently lost 40 pounds. I haven't lost enough—yet. But what I have lost, I have lost permanently.

Getting rid of your poor eating habits is a bit like quitting smoking. But there is a difference, too: you give up smoking completely and you do not give up eating completely. The best way to improve your eating habits permanently is to

70

change them slowly, one step at a time.

You cannot avoid knowing something about the caloric value of various foods. So buy a little calory-counter booklet the next time that you are in the grocery store or bookstore. You might get some surprises. But it is not necessary to carry a small balance around with you to weigh each portion—or a measuring cup to measure each serving.

It is necessary to think about eating. If you are obese, watch yourself eat. You cannot change your dietary habits if you do not know what you are changing. Observe yourself. You may be amazed to see what, and how much, you put into your mouth.

Then plan your changes. Plan them so that you wind up consuming what I have suggested: about 60 percent of your daily caloric intake from complex carbohydrates, about 20 percent from protein, and about 20 percent from fat. Compare what you are now eating to what you should be eating. For example, it may be that you are consuming about 50 percent of your calories from fat. If so, make some changes. If you are eating a sweet dessert every evening after dinner, switch to fresh fruit instead six days out of seven. (Go ahead and have a piece of cake after Sunday's dinner; just don't have one every day after dinner.)

And, almost certainly, you are consuming too many calories. Moderate your caloric intake. For example, if you have been eating two or three hamburgers for dinner, eat only one. If you drink half a dozen bottles of beer during the evening's TV watching, drink one or two. You need not radically change what you eat; it would be idiotic to go on a diet of, say, grapefruit and eggs. (But we Americans love idiotic diets!) Most obesity is caused by a simple imbalance between daily energy intake and expenditure. Eliminate the imbalance and you'll correct the obesity. An imbalance of just 100 calories a day (for example, ten potato chips or one light beer) can add ten pounds a year—or 100 pounds a decade. Looked at in this way, it is really not surprising that there are so many Americans who are obese after only two or three decades.

If this is correct, there are two practical pointers that follow. First, forget about your weight. Weigh yourself (if you must) not more than once a week. Your obesity is the result of overeating. Weighing yourself does not measure the problem, which is your overeating; it measures only the result. So frequent weigh-ins are unimportant. Second, lose weight slowly. I suggest that if you lose more than one half-pound per week on the average you are losing weight too rapidly. If you lose just one half-pound per week, you'll lose 26 pounds in a year (or 260 pounds in a decade!). Gentle, permanent improvements in your eating habits are better than radical, transitory ones. Slow weight loss will also enable your body to readjust to normal weight slowly; it will not greatly upset your metabolism. And you will adjust better to being lighter. I have noticed that, in some situations, it is better to have the heft of being fat than to lack it. For example, when I am pulling a boat out of a lake I miss those forty pounds. But such occasions are few and far between; usually, I am delighted at how much better I feel and look.

Avoid expecting too much too fast. If it took you four decades to become obese, it is idiotic to expect to be back to normal in four weeks. Take your time: no more than one half-pound per week. It is an attainable weekly goal for anyone. And savor the compliments that you'll receive. Enjoy looking younger. Enjoy feeling leaner. Celebrate a bit each time that you notch your belt one notch tighter. Look forward to your next physical exam when your physician will notice your permanent weight loss and the better results of your laboratory tests. Enjoy feeling a bit smug when you look at all those other frustrated people waddling through life!

If you need extra help, get it. Many of us have a problem with obesity. A lover or a friend can help. Support groups can help. Your physician can recommend some good books to read. Whatever it takes, commit yourself, daily, to doing it. And don't take it out in good intentions: do it!

It is also important to recognize when to stop. You should have a weight goal that you want to attain. Once attained, simply maintain it. Your physician can help you to set your ideal weight. You may wish to do it in terms of body fat. Cooper recommends that a man's body fat should never exceed 19 percent and that a woman's should never exceed 22 percent. (An athletic man's body fat should never exceed 15 percent and an athletic woman's should never exceed 18 percent.) He has developed a formula to translate these percentages into pounds. If you are a man of medium bone structure and want to calculate your approximate ideal weight at about a 15 to 19 percent body fat, multiply your height in inches by 4 and subtract 128. A woman should multiply her height in inches by 3.5 and subtract 108.[25] This calculation may be a bit extreme, so if you are within 5 or 10 pounds of it there probably isn't much to worry about. In my case, according to this, my ideal weight would be 168. But since I have a large bone structure, I would adjust it upward to about 175 or so. That's probably about right.

4. *Work to make your meals enjoyable.* My idea here is to

emphasize the quality instead of the quantity of what you eat.
It helps to have a good place for eating. If you have a dining
room with table and chairs, and perhaps some fine china and
crystal and a scenic view, that's terrific. Whatever place you
have, make it as attractive as possible. You may enjoy some
background music. You may enjoy some good conversation.
But make an effort to make your meal enjoyable. Don't take
out life's frustrations on yourself by overeating.

Take a bit of extra effort to make your meal look good as
well as taste good. For example, suppose that you are having
a half a grapefruit as part of your breakfast. Take a moment to prepare it properly. Take a grapefruit knife and slice
around each of the sections. Then take some kitchen shears
and cut out the white fiber in its center. Put a washed straw-
berry there and serve it on a plate with a grapefruit spoon.
Such care pays off in the long run.

And it is not just what sorts of foods are eaten, how much
food is eaten, and how food is prepared that is important.
When food is eaten is important. Concerning the timing of
meals, there are two widespread mistakes.

First, from a physiological point of view breakfast is the
most important meal of the day. It may have been 14 hours
since your body has received any nourishment. It may be that
you have a hard morning's work ahead of you. I have myself
seen otherwise intelligent people have just coffee and a
doughnut for breakfast! Get at least one-third of your daily
caloric intake at breakfast and, of course, balance the sorts of
nutrients that you are consuming properly. If you have been
failing to get a good breakfast, this single change alone could
cause you to become much more productive throughout the
morning, and you will probably start feeling much better in

just a week or two.

Second, from a physiological point of view the evening meal is the least important meal of the day. Food is your body's fuel. You do not normally fuel a machine after you run it; you fuel a machine before you run it. If you do most of your work during the day, it makes no sense whatsoever to eat a skimpy breakfast and a skimpy lunch and then a heavy evening meal. What will happen to all those evening calories? You won't expend them sitting around all evening. They'll tend to turn to fat. It makes much more sense to eat a hearty breakfast, a good lunch and a light supper.

Another common problem arises because of the fact that the midday meal is usually eaten away from home. It may not be practical to eat a well-balanced lunch. Breakfast and dinner may be less of a problem because they are eaten at home. But what should one have for lunch? My suggestion is to avoid fast-food hamburger joints and delicatessens and to make your own lunch and take it to work with you. There are two reasons for this. First, a lunch that you prepare yourself is likely to be lower in saturated fat and cholesterol than a lunch that you purchase in a fast food establishment. This is still true even though more and more of those establishments are making it somewhat easier to purchase a wholesome lunch. Second, a lunch that you prepare yourself is likely to be less expensive than a lunch that you purchase. Unless you are independently wealthy, this is a sufficient reason to avoid eating out on a daily basis. By all means go out to eat occasionally, but not more than once or twice a month. If you haven't prepared a lunch and want an inexpensive, wholesome meal, consider doing what I do in those circumstances:

simply buy and drink a quart of skim milk. So, after all this has been said, what might a typical day's menu look like?

BREAKFAST
1 small glass of orange juice
1/2 grapefruit
1/6 cantaloupe
Skim milk
High-fiber cereal with strawberries
Whole wheat toast
Banana
(Optional: coffee or tea)

LUNCH
Turkey sandwich on whole-wheat bread
Salad
Skim milk
Apple

DINNER
Steamed broccoli
Baked potato
Small serving of microwaved cod
Skim milk
Fresh fruit

What should one drink? The most important nutrient of all is water. Drink at least two quarts daily. Avoid substitutes. It is shocking that in 1984, for the first time, the most-consumed beverage in the U.S. was soft drinks instead of water. The only other nutritionally valuable fluids in addition to water are skim milk and fruit juice. Limit caffeine-containing beverages such as cola or coffee or tea to two servings daily—if you drink them at all.

This brings us to alcohol. If tobacco is not the most abused substance in North America today, alcohol is. From a caloric standpoint, one beer or a two-ounce cocktail or six ounces of wine contain 150 non-nutritive calories. So consumption of alcohol can produce unnecessary weight gains. And there are many other problems associated with the use of alcohol such as alcoholism, cirrhosis of the liver, and high blood pressure. Alcoholism is particularly insidious because it can creep up on drinkers without their being aware of it. If you have any suspicion at all that you may be a problem drinker, discuss it with your physician.[26] On the other hand, there has been some recent research that suggests that moderate amounts of alcohol (about 6 to 8 ounces per week) may have certain beneficial efforts on HDL levels in the blood. But such research should not be used as a license to drink freely.

If someone who can afford the calories has a drink before dinner, that person probably has no problem. But someone who has several drinks a day may have a problem. Someone who gets drunk once or twice a year may have no problem. But someone who gets drunk once or twice a week has a problem. If you suspect that you may have a problem, contact your physician.

Odds and ends: *i.* Starvation, which is occasionally recommended for the morbidly obese, is dangerous. It should therefore only be done under medical supervision. There is little evidence that total fasting results in more lasting weight reduction than a properly balanced, low-calory reducing diet.

ii. Intestinal bypass surgery should only be considered when the complications of the obesity itself are life-threatening and all other alternatives have failed to produce permanent weight loss.

iii. Appetite depressant drugs such as amphetamines are also dangerous. There seems to be no evidence that they are at all effective in producing permanent weight loss.

iv. Obesity becomes more of a problem with advancing age. So, even at the same energy expenditure level, do not expect to consume as many calories at age 50 as at age 25 without getting fatter. If you exercise moderately and are under 40, you may get a rough idea of the number of calories that you require daily just to meet your body's most basic requirements by multiplying your ideal weight by 15. For example, mine would be 175 x 15 or 2,625 calories. If you exercise strenuously, multiply your ideal weight by 20. If you don't exercise at all and are under 40, multiply your ideal weight by 12. If you are over 40 and exercise moderately, multiply your ideal weight by 13. If you are over forty and don't exercise at all, multiply your ideal weight by 10.[27] These figures may be a bit low, but they are probably not too far from ideal.

v. Maintaining an ideal weight is probably a factor in longevity. Have you ever seen many obese elderly persons?

vi. The 60/20/20 diet that I have suggested may reduce your chances of getting cancer. Recent studies have shown that obesity and a high intake of dietary fat are risk factors for certain kinds of cancer and that some vitamins and dietary fiber from fresh fruits and vegetables (especially those high in vitamins A and C such as grapefruit, oranges, nectarines, peaches, strawberries, cantaloupe, and honeydew melons)

melons) and from leafy green vegetables, yellow-orange vegetables (such as spinach, kale, sweet potatoes, carrots, cabbage, cauliflower, broccoli, and brussels sprouts) and yellow-orange fruits may help protect against certain kinds of cancer. Avoiding more than one or two alcoholic drinks a day also probably lowers your odds of getting certain kinds of cancer, namely, mouth, throat, liver, and esophagus cancer.

vii. Organically grown plants are not nutritionally superior to commercially fertilized plants. In fact, once they are removed from the field the two kinds cannot even be distinguished. But it is much better for the environment to grow plants organically, so you may want to reward the farmers who grow them organically by buying their produce even though it is more expensive.

viii. Salt is needed in the diet, but the natural salt that is already present in varying amounts in most foods is usually more than sufficient. Since the average American tends to add salt to foods, it is not surprising that many experts think that the average American's dietary salt intake, which is from 6 to 18 grams, is too high. A high amount of dietary salt is a risk factor for hypertension. So it is a good idea to stop adding salt automatically to everything. If you do, your tastes are likely to change quickly, to adjust to a more appropriate level of dietary salt intake.

ix. The walking exercise program that I suggest in the next chapter involves walking briskly, in other words, walking at a pace that covers four miles each hour. Anyone who exercises by walking briskly expends about 475 calories per hour.

5
Exercise and Recovery

The idea of health is not the same as the idea of fitness. The idea of health is the idea of being free from disease, the symptoms of disease, or injury. The idea of fitness is chiefly the idea of cardiovascular fitness: you are fit when the bodily systems that are responsible for the transportation and utilization of oxygen operate with a high degree of efficiency. Like the idea of health ('healthy', 'healthier', 'healthiest'), the idea of fitness ('fit', 'fitter', 'fittest') is comparative; it comes in degrees. But this should not obscure the four possible ways to classify a person with respect to health and fitness: healthy and fit, unhealthy and fit, healthy and unfit, and unhealthy and unfit.

It is better to be fit than unfit. Just as someone who is healthy is able to be more productive than someone who is unhealthy, someone who is fit is able to be more productive than someone who is unfit. Perhaps because I am an ex-soldier, I always think of battle in these cases. If I found myself in a battle, would I want my commander to be healthy or unhealthy, fit or unfit? Obviously, anyone would prefer a healthy, fit commander. When the chips are down, when human life is on the line, it is better to be healthy and fit than to fall into any of the other three categories. There is an obvious sense in which your life is on the line at every moment. It is certainly on the line during some emergencies and during some extremely stressful moments.

There is evidence that being fit contributes to being healthy and that being fit improves the quality of life. All other things being equal, a fit person is likely to have the following advantages over an unfit person: a higher level of energy for longer periods; a stronger, healthier bone structure; improved digestion; and improved sleep. A fit person is less likely than an unfit person to suffer from such ailments as heart disease, obesity, constipation, depression, and emotional disturbance. A healthy, fit person is likely to live longer than a person who is unhealthy, unfit, or both. A fit woman is less likely than an unfit woman to have severe problems of menstruation. A fit person is more likely than an unfit person to feel better every day—though the only evidence here is anecdotal.

As with your health, your fitness is not entirely in your control. But you can improve your chances of being healthy by eliminating physical habits with deleterious effects on your health (for example, smoking) and by developing physical habits with beneficial effects on your health (for example, eating a properly balanced and prepared variety of foods). Likewise, you can improve your chances of being fit by exercising. Most persons, even those confined to a wheelchair, can get some exercise and thereby improve their fitness.

I know of no good argument against exercising to improve fitness. Most such arguments are based on false beliefs (and may be motivated by physical laziness). For example, some people believe that exercise increases appetite and that they will tend to get fat if they exercise. The truth is that moderate exercise has very little effect on appetite, and strenuous exercise actually decreases appetite. Some people believe that exercising is dangerous. The truth is that a properly planned program of moderate exercise is not particularly dangerous. Failing to exercise is more dangerous than exercising properly. Some people believe that exercising takes time that could be better spent working on one's Project. Exercising does take time—at least 90 minutes a week, but spending those 90 minutes exercising will actually increase your ability to work hard on your Project. Furthermore, there is important recent evidence that suggests that, since exercising tends to prolong life, you will get back later all those hours that you now devote to exercising. On the other hand, there is such a thing as too much exercise, a point at which the costs outweigh the benefits. But most of us ought to increase, not decrease, our amount of exercise.

All adult multicelled organisms grow old and die. In this sense we are all deteriorating slightly every day. We are steadily aging. Someone who is unfit or unhealthy is likely to be deteriorating at a faster rate than someone who is fit and healthy. What exercise is able to do is to retard (and, perhaps, even temporarily reverse) the inexorable process of deterioration. If this is correct, you would expect, for example, that a fit, fifty-year-old person would feel younger than an unfit, fifty-year-old person. And this is just what you do seem to find. It is impossible, of course, to compare directly their bodily 'feels'. But, by exercising, it is possible to go from being unfit to fit (and, by not exercising, from being fit to unfit)—and I have never met anyone who preferred the 'feels' of being unfit to the 'feels' of being fit.

I should emphasize that I am dealing in this book only

with beliefs that are rational, probably true, as opposed to beliefs that are certainly true, to knowledge. Since the consequences of an action are relevant to its moral worth and since it is impossible to know all the consequences of an action in advance, it is not possible to know whether an action is right or wrong in advance.[28] But the fundamental assumption of this book is that we are able to have rational beliefs about the consequences of our actions and, as Plato points out, with respect to acting (as opposed to merely understanding), a true belief that something is the case is every bit as good as knowing that it is the case.

Someone usually points out during the course of this argument what I think of as 'the Winston Churchill factor.' Imagine a ninety-year-old man who has just died. Imagine that he felt terrific throughout his life, that he had been enormously productive, that he never exercised (or regularly engaged in physical labor), that he had several physical habits with deleterious health effects (suppose, for example, that he was an alcoholic who drank a fifth of whisky daily and was a heavy cigarette smoker), and that he had few physical habits with beneficial health effects (suppose, for example, that he normally failed to eat a properly balanced variety of foods and that he had been grossly obese because of regular overeating). The truth is that a few such people exist. What about them?

In terms of the longevity statistics alone, probably 10 percent of the population will die young and probably 10 percent of the population will die old regardless of their physical habits. If so, that still leaves four out of five of us for whom the development of good physical habits may increase longevity. The man imagined in the previous paragraph would simply be one of the lucky ones.

Notice that the argument may be turned around: our imagined man was lucky to live so long and to feel so good. Perhaps his drinking, smoking, inactivity, and over-eating were what made his life tolerable! But how do we know that he might not have lived even longer if he had developed good physical habits? And how do we know that he might not have felt even better if he had developed good physical habits? Notice that Winston Churchill himself was unproductive and ill in his old age. If he had developed better physical habits he might well have been even more productive and healthier than he was, and he might have lived longer than he actually did. The best current evidence suggests that a life span of about 115 years is natural; in other words, the human body will eventually wear out but there is no known reason why it must wear out before 11 or 12 decades. So perhaps Churchill missed about a quarter of a century of living.

There are three main questions concerning exercise as a means to fitness. 1. What is the best kind of exercise? 2. How much exercise is sufficient? 3. What is the best way to get a sufficient amount of the best kind of exercise?

1. There are five chief types of exercise.[29] *i. Isometric exercise* involves contracting a muscle or muscle group, but does not involve motion of any part of the body. For example, if you stand in a doorway, place the outsides of your hands on the insides of the doorjambs, and press outward as hard as possible for ten seconds, you have done an isometric exercise. It is possible to increase muscle size and strength with isometric exercises. However, isometric exercise has little or no effect on the cardiovascular system and, so, cannot improve your fitness. *ii. Isotonic (or isophasic) exercise* involves contracting a muscle or muscle group and requires moving (working, stressing) some part or parts of the body against resistance (usually gravity)—primarily in one direction. For example, if you grab an overhead bar with both hands, with your arms straight, and then pull yourself upward until your chin is higher than the bar, you have done an isotonic exercise. All calisthenics and lifting of free weights (weights unattached to a weight machine) are isotonic exercises. Isotonic exercise is a good way to increase muscle size and strength (or 'bulk and power' as the bodybuilders say). But, even though it may leave you gasping for breath, isotonic exercise has little or no effect on the cardiovascular system (because it does not last long enough). *iii. Isokinetic exercise* involves contracting a muscle or muscle group and involves moving some part or parts of the body against resistance in both directions. For example, doing a chin-up requires work in only one direction, namely, when you are pulling yourself up. Even if you do it slowly, it is easy to lower yourself down again. Imagine a machine that was so constructed that you would work in both directions (up and down) when doing a chin-up. Using such a machine would be doing an isokinetic exercise. Again, even though it may leave you gasping for breath, isokinetic exercise has little or no effect on the cardiovascular system (because it does not last long enough).

It is possible to improve your fitness, however, by using a series of isotonic or isokinetic exercises. If you move without resting from one weight station or machine to the next and continue in this way for a while (doing a 'giant set' or 'superset' or 'circuit' or 'supercircuit'), then it is possible to improve your fitness because you make the whole sequence of exercises (which don't last long enough individually) last long enough. However invaluable a specific isotonic or isokinetic exercise is for developing strength, it is an *iv. anaerobic exercise,* one without oxygen. A sequence of them may become *v. aerobic,* an exercise with oxygen. In an *anaerobic exercise,* a person does not utilize the oxygen that is being breathed during the exercise. For example, someone who sprints 100 yards is exercising anaerobically. A sprinter could run the entire distance without breathing. Even if he does breathe during the sprint, he is not using the oxygen that is being breathed during the sprint. In an *aerobic exercise,* a person utilizes the oxygen that is being breathed during the exercise. For example, someone who runs a marathon is exercising aerobically. The marathon runner is obviously using the oxygen that is being breathed during the exercise; the marathon runner is exercising at a steady state. It takes a while to reach this steady state: someone who runs a mile may be exercising half-anaerobically and half-aerobically. This is why an exercise must last a sufficient amount of time to be an aerobic exercise. How much time? It depends upon the fitness level of the person exercising. But any exercise that lasts less than about 8 or 10 minutes probably will not qualify as aerobic.

Aerobic exercise increases the efficiency of the functioning of the bodily systems that are responsible for the transportation and utilization of oxygen. Oxygen enters the bloodstream through the lungs and the heart circulates the blood. It is this cardiovascular system that is improved by aerobic exercise. The capacity of the lungs increases and there is some evidence that such an increase is associated with greater longevity. The total blood volume in the body increases and this increase means that the body is better equipped to transport oxygen, which means greater endurance. The heart

87

muscle itself improves: it gets stronger, becomes better supplied with blood, and increases its stroke volume. The benefit of improving, say, your biceps (by strengthening and enlarging them) pales in importance when compared to the benefits of improving your cardiovascular system. It is for this reason that aerobic exercise is the best kind of exercise.

2. How much aerobic exercise is sufficient? The experts disagree on the exact amount. But most seem to think that three 30-minute periods of strenuous aerobic exercise per week are sufficient. Only 90 minutes a week!

3. What is the best way to get a sufficient amount of aerobic exercise? It depends upon the individual. There are many different sorts of aerobic exercises: swimming, running or jogging, walking, cross-country skiing, outdoor cycling, skating, aerobic dancing, or playing games such as handball, racketball, squash, basketball, or hockey, to name only a few. But let us begin at the beginning.

If you are over 30, the beginning is to obtain your physician's approval (based on a comprehensive physical examination) before starting any regimen of aerobic exercise. If you are under 30 and are in good health, you need not obtain your physician's approval.

The next step is to choose a basic aerobic exercise. Choose exactly one and match it as closely as possible to your individual situation. The exercise that you pick should meet two conditions. First, it should be an activity that you are able to do year-round. If you live in Texas, forget cross-country skiing. If you live in upstate New York and don't have access to an indoor pool, forget swimming. Second, it should be an activity that will enable you to keep your cardiovascular system working hard for 30 consecutive minutes. If you enjoy golf or horseback riding, for example, do it in addition to your basic aerobic exercise—not instead of it. Of course, if you have a basic aerobic exercise that you are interested in and that you enjoy, terrific!

But most North Americans are unfit. Judging from their behavior, they simply do not enjoy aerobic exercise. If most people had an aerobic exercise that they enjoyed, presumably they would do it. Since they aren't doing it, I presume that they haven't one that they sufficiently enjoy. Since getting started on a regular program of aerobic exercise is the most difficult part, permit me to make some suggestions based on my own experience.[30]

How to begin. Suppose that your physician has told you that it will be safe for you to begin a program of aerobic exercise. And suppose that you understand the benefits of such a program and have even been thinking about it for some time. What next?

Pick an exercise and commit yourself to it for ten weeks. Whatever else you do for the next ten weeks, stick to your program. If need be, pretend that exercise is like bad medicine. Pretend that you won't begin to feel and to look better. Pretend that you won't be any healthier. Pretend that it will be nothing but a waste of time for ten weeks, but that it is simply something that you must do. In other words, assume the worst. Assume that you won't enjoy it at all. In fact, assume that you will hate it. (Then, if you do hate it, you won't be surprised.) After a while, you may secretly start to enjoy it. But, at the beginning, wipe any thought of enjoyment from your mind. You have decided to exercise because you believe in being fit. Period.

Permit me to pick an exercise. (I need an example,

anyway.) I suggest walking. Almost everyone is capable of walking. It doesn't matter how old you are. It doesn't matter which sex you are. It doesn't matter where you live. It doesn't require any special equipment. It can be done year-round. In fact, it has, at most, two disadvantages. First, it is time-consuming. It will take more than 90 minutes weekly. But since it does not require going anywhere and since it does not require much warm-up or cool-down, it is not as time-consuming as you might think. Furthermore, if you don't have a partner to talk with, you can always think (plan, dream) during a walk or, at least, simply enjoy being outdoors. This leads to the second possible disadvantage. We have so fouled the air, at least in our large cities, that exercising outdoors can sometimes be hazardous to your health. If this is a problem in your neighborhood, walk only when air pollution levels are low (and support politicians who support clean air legislation).

Walking tends to tighten up the back of the body, so you would be wise to stretch for two or three minutes even before going on a simple walk. Stretch, briefly, at least the Achilles' tendons, the hamstrings, the groin muscles, and the lower back. If you do not know how to stretch, find out. Buy a book on how-to-stretch in a bookstore or sporting goods store. They are inexpensive and readily available. Study the pictures and read the descriptions carefully. Practice stretching and concentrate on how you feel as you are stretching. Do not, for example, allow yourself to be distracted; pay attention or you may pull a muscle. Never bounce. Hold the stretch for 15 to 30 seconds and go on to the next stretch. With a little practice, you should be able to complete your stretching for walking in less than three minutes.

Dress sensibly. Jogging shoes are the best, but any sturdy shoe with some heel cushioning is acceptable. Wear clean white socks. And dress in layers so that, if you get too warm, you'll be able to peel off a layer as you walk.

Walk nonstop. The goal, after ten weeks of working up to it, is: two miles in less than 30 minutes six times a week. That's all. Here's a progressive chart.

week	distance in miles	time in minutes
1	0.5	10
2	1	24
3	1.5	34
4	2	40
5	2	39
6	2	38
7	2	36
8	2	34
9	2	32
10	2	30

Walk six days per week. Reach the time goal at the end of the week. For example, by the end (not the beginning) of the fourth week you should be able to cover the two mile distance in 40 minutes. Once you are able to walk two miles in less than 30 minutes six times a week, *keep at it for at least six months.* This program will keep you decently fit—although, of course, you won't be able to go out and run a marathon. But that is not the point. The point is to get regular, moderate exercise and that is what this program is.

Before mentioning how to improve to an intermediate

level, let me pass along a few training tips that may make your walking easier.

Don't get ahead of the chart if you have not been exercising regularly. You may be able to make the time and mileage goal the first or second week, but, since your body is not accustomed to regular exercise, you may not be able to sustain it. Give yourself a break! Progress slowly—along with the chart. There is no rush. Take it easy. Exercising should not be painful. It has probably taken years of deconditioning to get into your present condition, so it is surely sensible to give your body a mere ten weeks in which to turn around.

If you ever develop any unusual symptoms, stop exercising immediately. Get your physician's advice before continuing.

Schedule a regular time for exercising—and let nothing short of injury or fever stop you from exercising. *Never skip a workout* during the first ten weeks. Never let an exception occur until your new habit of walking is well-established. (Once it is well-established, you will probably not want to miss a workout.)

There are three good times to workout: i. in the morning, ii. at midday, and iii. before supper. Pick one of the three times and stay with it for the initial ten week period. *i.* The chief advantage to working out *in the morning* is that you get your workout over with. You do not permit yourself to develop excuses during the day for not doing it. It has an initial priority on your life that no other activity has. It is the best time for a beginner to work out. Furthermore, you'll feel better for the rest of the day. And air pollution levels are likely to be lower in the early morning than later in the day. There are several minor disadvantages to working out in the morning. First, you have to get up a bit earlier and, so, ought to go to sleep a bit earlier. Second, your body may be stiff in the morning. It may take a bit of extra time to get limber. So don't just hop out of bed and start stretching. Putter around for at least 20 minutes to allow your muscles and tendons to warm up naturally. Third, in northern climates it can be dark in the morning; this can make it dangerous to walk along a road. But if you are quite familiar with the road and wear reflective clothing, it need not be very dangerous. *ii.* If you have an hour *lunch break* at work, that's a good time to walk (at least on weekdays). By then your body will be naturally limber and it is a regular break that can be used for exercising. It may not be difficult to get a fellow worker or two to walk with you. And, unless you live in the far north, there is always enough daylight at lunch time. Stretching, walking, and then eating lunch can easily be done in an hour. *iii.* Another good time to exercise is *before supper.* Throughout the workday you'll probably have accumulated stress at work and, by exercising, you'll be able to relieve that stress and set yourself up for an enjoyable evening. Furthermore, if you exercise just before your evening meal it is likely that you'll eat a lighter meal. The chief disadvantage to exercising before supper is that you will have had all day to dream up some excuse for not exercising. For this reason, I do not suggest that you work out before supper until you are through your initial ten-week period. If your job involves physical labor, you should work out before your work day begins; otherwise, you may be too tired.

People often con themselves about not having the time to exercise. But think of it this way: we all manage to find enough time to sleep because sleeping is mandatory. Exercising is mandatory, too. Make the time for it. We all find

93

enough time to eat because eating is mandatory. Think of exercising as being mandatory, too. Walking those two miles is mandatory—and any additional exercise that you happen to get during the day is simply a bonus.

Think about your exercising the day before you do it. Visualize yourself walking and completing your walk. Tell yourself at night that the one thing you are going to do tomorrow is to walk those two miles. It sounds silly, but it will help you develop the habit.

If it helps, get a dog and walk with it. You know that the dog needs regular exercise. So you can get your regular exercise while you are walking your dog. If you are able to afford one, you may want to purchase a motorized treadmill and walk on it. You can get your exercise while watching your favorite TV program!

You need not shower after a walk. It is nervous perspiration that smells—not healthy sweat.[31] Strip off your exercise clothes and simply towel dry before dressing your in street clothes again. This can save time during a lunch break. Of course, if you take a daily bath or shower, you may well want to take it after your walk

Give yourself one complete day of rest per week. Walk six days, not seven.

Find a way to motivate yourself to walk on days when you simply don't feel like it. This is the chief advantage of walking with a partner or in a group: you won't want to let your partner(s) down. Your aerobic exercise will form your conditioning base for other games and sports, and you may be able to use this as a motivational factor. For example, suppose that you are in a bowling league. Tell yourself that your walking will benefit your bowling and that you are walking for the good of your bowling team. It doesn't matter if this is false. We have the ability to turn the process of rationalization around, so *use reverse rationalization* to work for you. Tell yourself that your sex life will improve. (It may.) Or think of someone to walk for. Walk for your spouse. Or walk for someone you don't even know. Professional athletes have to perform at the peak of their physical abilities over and over again when they certainly don't feel like it. How do they do it? Some of them do it by picking someone to play for. Bill Bradley and Dave DeBusschere were teammates on the New York Knickerbockers professional basketball team. Here is Bradley's account of the player introductions before a game.

> DuBusschere and I stand stonefaced as the remaining introductions are made. DeBusschere says, "I found her. I'm playing for her tonight."
> "Where, which one?" I ask.
> "The blonde in the blue sweater up to the right of Gate 13."
> I glance up . . . until I focus on an unknown woman in a gray skirt and a blue turtleneck sweater. She gazes down at us as the National Anthem is announced. "Okay, we'll do it for her tonight," I say.[32]

They didn't even need to see her ever again; all they needed was someone to perform for. Find someone or something to motivate you and walk.

It is good to walk on level ground. But if you find yourself walking along, say, a suburban road, notice that the road surface is crowned, that it slopes down from the center on both sides. If you therefore walk your two miles facing traffic, you'll be walking the whole way on a surface that slopes down to the left. For this reason, it is better to walk one mile with traffic and one mile against traffic. Since walking with traffic can be dangerous, it is a good idea to keep as far from the center of the road as possible and to wear something reflective.

If your course includes hills, understand that you never regain going downhill the extra energy that you have expended going uphill. You can balance the two by the simple expedient of going in one direction for the first mile and then retracing your steps for the second mile.

What about your house or apartment key? If you happen to wear lightweight running shorts, they may have a key pocket—but don't use it. Eventually your key will poke a hole through the pocket and you'll lose it. Instead, slip your key over the lace of one shoe before you tie it.

It is not a good idea to carry a radio with you—or to use headphones. You should be able to hear approaching traffic or barking dogs in order to avoid them. (Nearly all dogs can be scared off by simply picking up a stone and holding it over your head as if you were going to throw it. But throw it if you need to.)

If you are able to afford one, consider buying a Gore-Tex running suit. It will keep you dry when it rains (unlike a cotton sweat suit) and it will breathe (unlike a nylon or rubber suit). Whatever top you choose in cool or cold weather, it should have a zippered front to allow you to make adjustments as your body warms up during your exercise. Unlined, seam-sealed Gore-Tex mittens are an inexpensive luxury for cold weather.

It is best to walk on a soft surface (grass or firm sand is better than concrete or asphalt), but it is better to walk on a hard surface than not to walk at all. If you have a tendency toward shin splints, you may be able to make some positive changes. Try a good pair of running shoes; they offer the best cushion and support. Try finding a softer surface to walk on. Try losing weight. Try walking backwards for a quarter-mile or so after your walk; this will help develop your muscles in the other direction. Try exercises that strengthen the muscles in your shins (for example, lifting the front of your feet and spreading and gripping the floor with your toes or walking back and forth across your living room on your heels).

Avoid as much as possible exercising in hot, humid, sunny weather. Avoid working out during one's lunch break in the summertime—switch to an early morning or late afternoon workout. Even if such times are not less humid, they will be a bit cooler and the rays of the sun will be less direct. There is no particular problem with cool or cold weather: it is, for example, much easier to exercise at 20 degrees Farenheit than at 80 degrees Farenheit. But try to avoid working up a sweat in cool or cold weather—open up your sweatshirt before you develop a good sweat. If you don't, you may get chilled. I do not suggest outside workouts when it is colder than –20 degrees Farenheit or hotter than 95 degrees Farenheit.

Let me again emphasize the importance of keeping at the two-mile distance for six months. It is not wise to try to exceed it. If you have been sedentary for decades, it is foolish to expect overnight results.

If after six months, you really enjoy your new fitness, you may want a bit more. One way is to increase the frequency of your walks. Suppose, for example, that you walk Monday through Saturday mornings. Try also walking on Monday, Wednesday, and Friday afternoons. Instead of six walks weekly, you'll be getting nine. Or walk twice a day for twelve times a week. You'll be exercising twice as much as you need to, but you'll be fitter than you would otherwise be.

Another alternative is to increase your distance. This may allow you to decrease the frequency of your walks. Cooper recommends one of the following:[33]

frequency per week	distance in miles	maximum time
5	4.0	80 minutes
4	3.0	45 minutes
3	4.0	60 minutes

Any of these programs will give you a better workout than the two-mile program—and they may be more convenient. Any one of them will give you a sufficient amount of aerobic exercise. In addition, you'll be burning up about 475 calories per hour and this may well be the difference between your gaining and losing several pounds during the year.

This amount of exercise will also form a decent aerobic base for more strenuous activities if you want to engage in them. You may, for example, want to go cross-country skiing some lovely winter day—or for a swim on a hot summer's day. On such days, you need not do your walking.

How to reach an intermediate level. Walking may not be enough exercise to satisfy you. It is possible to build a better aerobic base than any of the walking programs just mentioned. Let me stress, however, that any of the walking programs is sufficient to maintain minimal fitness. If you want the minimum, choose one, make it part of your daily routine, and skip the rest of this chapter.

Running (or jogging) is preferable to walking for some people because the same aerobic benefit can be derived about three times more quickly. Running, however, is harder on the body than walking. Some changes should, therefore, be made. Let me recommend an intermediate running program and then make a few further suggestions about how to proceed on from there. My assumption is that you have been walking for at least six months. I do *not* suggest any running (for any sedentary person over the age of 15) without a successful six-month walking program. It may simply be too hard for your body, which increases the likelihood that you'll quit. It is better to build upon success. Once you have maintained a successful walking program for six months, you are ready to go on to something more strenuous should you choose to do so (although, from the point of view of fitness, there is no need to do so). It is important to plan to be successful.

There are three parts to any satisfactory intermediate-level exercise program: stretching for flexibility, aerobic exercising for fitness, and improving muscular strength. Of course, there are other excellent exercises (for example, cross-country skiing, swimming, and outdoor cycling) that may be pursued in place of running. But all require special equipment and weather conditions. Since running only requires a good pair of running shoes, permit me to use it as an example.

If you have not already done so for the walking program, go to a well-stocked sporting goods store and buy a good pair of running shoes. It helps if you get a salesman who knows what he is talking about. If you are not satisfied, try another store. Two further points about your shoes. First, replace them once a year or every 500 miles, whichever comes first, because their ability to absorb the shock of running decreases with use. Second, you may require heel wedges. Stand with bare feet on a hard floor and have someone look at your Achilles' tendons. Are they straight? If so, fine. If not, if they bow slightly in (as they most often do) or slightly out, you should add rubber heel wedges to your shoes to straighten your tendons. These are available at shoe repair shops and in well-stocked drug stores. If you need them and don't add them, you may wind up with knee problems.

Pay particular attention to the suggestions that I made about walking. For example, never run for miles on a surface that tilts in one direction or I guarantee that you'll eventually have knee problems. Never run in the dark: if you happen to land on a stone or the edge of the road pavement, you could twist an ankle or a knee, or even fall. (And, of course, it is difficult for drivers to see a runner in the dark.) Try running backwards for a while after your run to balance your muscular development and to prevent shin splints.

i. The first step is to shift from a walking program to a running or jogging program without increasing the amount of exercise that you are getting. ii. The second step is to increase the amount of exercise.

i. To shift successfully from a six-day-a-week walking program to a six-day-a-week running program, try the following. By the end of the first week (in other words, after six running sessions), you should be able to cover one mile in 10 minutes or less. By the end of the second week, you should be able to cover one mile in 9 minutes or less. By the end of the third week, you should be able to cover one mile in 8 minutes or less. So, after three weeks, you will be running one mile in 8 minutes or less six times a week.

You will probably find that this is a bit harder on your body than walking. (For this reason, you should never run a mile faster than 7 minutes per mile even if you are able to do so. Increasing your pace increases the pounding and risk of injury. The additional aerobic benefit is not worth the greater risk of injury.) I know that I do; so I never run six days a week. I suggest a three-day-a-week running schedule. This will give your body at least 48 hours to recover completely from your previous run. Therefore, once you are able to run a mile in 8 minutes or less six times a week, I suggest that you go to the following three-day-a-week schedule: run two miles in 16 minutes or less. Even at this point, however, you will still be getting only about the same amount of aerobic exercise that you used to get on one of the walking programs.

ii. If you now want to increase the amount of exercise that you are getting, it is easy to do so. Basically all you need to do is increase your mileage (and, hence, the time that your exercise takes); you need not run faster. If you have spent

frequency per week	distance in miles	maximum time
3	2.5	25 minutes
3	3.0	35 minutes
3	3.0	30 minutes
3	3.5	36 minutes
3	4.0	48 minutes
3	4.0	40 minutes
3	4.5	45 minutes
3	5.0	60 minutes
3	5.0	50 minutes

three weeks shifting from a walking to a running program and one week shifting from a six-day-a-week program to a three-day-a-week program and want to go on, try the following. Start with the program on the top line. If you wish to do more, go down one line. You may stay indefinitely with the program at any line.

Any of these programs is a very good one. Anyone who runs 9 or 12 or 15 miles a week at about a nine-minute-mile pace will be able to satisfy anyone's definition of fitness. Unless you are a competitive athlete, there is never any reason to run more than 15 miles a week. In fact, even at 15 miles a week the injury rate may be too high. Twelve miles a week is less hard on the body and will provide nearly as much aerobic benefit.

These programs are likely to be sustained indefinitely, however, only if you take care to warm up and to cool down properly. Never try any of these programs without a good warm up and a proper cool down.

A good warm up involves stretching. Stretching by itself is beneficial. Even if you do no aerobic exercise, you are likely to feel better if you stretch daily than if you don't. Furthermore, stretching may provide some protection from injury. Stretching will make your body loose, supple, limber. Someone who is loose and, say, slips on a patch of ice in the winter may more likely have the bodily confidence to roll with the fall and to bounce up uninjured than someone who is tight, although my evidence here is only anecdotal.

A runner should use his stretching book to develop a thorough, individual stretching program. Each of us has a slightly different build. For this reason, I may find a certain

102

stretch that someone else recommends either impossible or too painful to be beneficial. Develop for yourself a comprehensive program. Three minutes of proper stretching is probably satisfactory for a walking program; it may not be satisfactory for a running program. Your stretching program should take at least 15 minutes. And, say, if early November darkness leaves you with no time in the afternoon both to stretch and to run, don't run. Wait until the next day when you have time for both. I never run without stretching and I have never injured myself running.[34]

The best sort of warm-up also gets your heart pumping a bit faster. I suggest jogging in place or running in a circle for a minute or two before stretching.

It's a good idea to cool down after your run. Walk for a minute or so and then jog for about a quarter of a mile. I then always walk and jog a ways backwards (for a total of at least a quarter of a mile).

What about the other workout days? I suggest the following. First, do your usual pre-run stretching. Second, do a sequence of three strengthening exercises. As any well-conditioned athlete can confirm, a strong mid-section is crucial. So the strengthening exercises should work our physical centers.

i. Abdominal work. There is no substitute for sit-ups for strengthening stomach muscles. There are different ways to do sit-ups. What is important is working the five groups of abdominal muscles without injuring the back. Choose either of the following methods; the first is a bit easier to do than the second, though I prefer the second.

METHOD 1: Lie with the calves of your legs on the seat of

a kitchen chair and your back on the floor. Your thighs should be perpendicular to the floor and should remain perpendicular to the floor during the exercise. Clasp your hands loosely behind your head. Contract your abdominal muscles and slowly pull your head as close to your knees as possible and go back down. That is one repetition. Do not cheat. Do not, for example, pull with your hands on the back of your head— or throw your elbows forward as you arise. Do the movement strictly. If you are able at first to do only one or two repetitions correctly, it doesn't matter. If you do your best by working until failure (in other words, until you are unable to do even one more repetition) each workout, you'll soon be doing 20 or 50 or 100 repetitions. (Unless you want a 'washboard' stomach, there is never a reason to exceed 100 repetitions.)

METHOD 2: Lie on the floor on your back with your legs straight, your feet together, and your arms crossed over your chest. Curl slowly upward: raise your torso off the floor while simultaneously raising your legs while bending your knees. When your knees meet the top of your chest, lower yourself slowly to the starting position making sure to rest the back of your heels on the floor. Do one set until failure.

Whichever method you choose, do the sit-ups slowly and correctly. It is always better to do fewer repetitions correctly than more repetitions incorrectly.

ii. Back work. Lie on the floor on your stomach with your legs straight, your feet together (toes pointed), your arms folded, and your chin resting on the top of your hands. Curl slowly upward: raise your torso off the floor while simultaneously raising your legs without bending your knees. Raise only as high as you can comfortably go. Hold at the top for two seconds and lower yourself slowly to the starting position. Do one set until comfortably tired.

This exercise works the muscles of the lower back, the buttocks, and the hamstrings. It may be too difficult if your back is very weak. If so, for a few weeks do the exercise without raising your legs (in other words, only raise your torso).

iii. Upper-body work. There are many good exercises that work the five major muscle groups of the upper torso. These muscle groups are the shoulders, the chest, the upper back, the triceps, and the biceps. Probably the best exercise without equipment (such as barbells or parallel bars or exercise machines), and one that almost everyone knows how to do correctly, is the push-up.

Lie on the floor on your stomach with your legs straight, your feet together, and the palms of your hands on the floor just outside your shoulders. Reach the starting position by keeping your back straight and raising yourself until your body is parallel to the floor with all your weight resting on your toes and on the palms of your hands. Push yourself up by locking your arms while keeping your back straight; lower yourself slowly until your chest just touches the floor. That is one repetition. Do one set until failure.

Again, it doesn't matter if you are only able to do one or two repetitions in the beginning. If you work until failure each workout, you'll soon be doing 20 or 50 or 100. When you reach this point, make your exercise more difficult by, for example, doing them on closed fists or on fingertips or on three, sturdy, hard chairs.

105

A very good intermediate level program, then, would wind up looking something like this:

Monday **Wednesday** **Friday**	warm-up stretch 3-mile run in under 30 minutes proper cool-down
Tuesday **Thursday** **Saturday**	warm-up stretch one set of sit-ups one set of back exercises one set of push-ups
Sunday	complete physical rest

It is possible to get a greater degree of cardiovascular fitness. Anyone wishing to do so should first work up to doing the five-mile run in under 50 minutes three times a week. On the other three workout days, add interval training, which involves a series of faster, shorter runs. (Even marathon runners regularly use interval training.) One might, for example, do several 880s (half-mile runs), several 440s, and several 220s. But this sort of training is only for competitive athletes.

It is also possible to get stronger. Overall body strength is largely determined by the strength of the largest muscle groups, namely, the thighs and the back. To increase overall body strength, therefore, you need to exercise your thighs and back. To do this on free weights, for example, you should do squats and (bent-knee) deadlifts. However, these exercises are dangerous for persons who do not know exactly what they are doing. Serious isotonic or isokinetic exercise is only needed by competitive athletes. But if you are interested, I suggest joining a gym for a month or two. Most gyms have relatively inexpensive introductory programs. The best offer both isotonic and isokinetic equipment. If you enjoy your workouts in the gym, you can either make going to the gym a regular habit or purchase your own equipment and use it at home. But, for most people, the exercises that I suggested will be sufficient over the long term.

An alternative program that I like is a simple three day rotation. Essentially, you run on the first day, workout on weights the second day, and rest the third day.

It is not a good idea to exercise if there is something wrong with your body. If you have a fever or a muscle pull or a slight sprain, rest. Many people want to imitate the professional or serious amateur athletes that they see on TV; they want to train or to compete even when in pain. But remember that such athletes are in excellent condition, regularly get the best available medical care, and have only a few years in which to compete at the highest level. I am discussing exercise habits that will be good for a lifetime. A common cold should not, however, restrict your exercise program.

You'll probably learn to avoid drinking any fluid in the half-hour or so before a run. Otherwise, it may slosh around in your stomach. I recommend that you avoid drinking any alcohol in the 24 hours prior to a run; 48 hours is better. (If you are a competitive athlete, the 24-hour rule should also be observed before practices as well as before games—and 48 hours is better.)

It's a good idea to avoid eating for two hours prior to running; otherwise, the food in your stomach may give you a 'stitch' in your abdomen. As one ages, it is wise to extend this rule. For example, I eat my pregame meal four hours before a hockey game. If I violate this rule, I feel sluggish on the ice.

Pay attention to your body. Most heart attacks, for example, do give warnings. Stop exercising if you feel any of the following symptoms: sharp chest pain, chest discomfort, 'heavy' (crushing) pain under the breastbone, strange pains (for example, jaw pain, arm pain, neck pain, throat pain, or stomach pain), any dizziness, nausea, excessive fatigue, exhaustion, or malaise. If any of these symptoms recur in the same place, consult your physician immediately. On the other hand, regular, moderate exercise such as I have suggested has recently been shown to reduce the overall chances of death from heart disease by 30-50 percent.

You should expect to suffer from certain minor injuries from time to time. You may, for example, occasionally pull muscles while stretching. And when you are injured, rest. Your physician can advise you on the best way to treat minor injuries. Or you can do your own research in the library. There are a number of available books that provide generally good advice (for example, Don H. O'Donoghue's *Treatment of Injuries to Athletes*, or Steven Roy and Richard Irvin's *Sports Medicine: Prevention, Evaluation, Management, and Rehabilitation*, or Otto Appenzeller and Ruth Atkinson, eds., *Sports Medicine: Fitness, Training, Injuries*—although such works are likely to benefit physicians more than nonphysicians).

There may be some columnists in your local newspaper who offer sound advice (for example, though a former professional athlete and not a physician, Pat McInally's judgment is usually good). And when you are well enough to resume exercising, go slowly. Do not expect to pick up where you left off. Deliberately drop back to a lower level, even to a walking program, and slowly build back to where you were.

Even at an intermediate level of running you can benefit from tips from more advanced runners. For example, you can easily avoid dry skin rubbing against dry skin (and the resulting chafes, irritation, and blisters) by putting some petroleum jelly between your toes, inner upper thighs, and near your armpits. The *Wellness Letter* is a source of such tips. Another is *Runner's World* magazine.

It is important to recover properly from exercise. In addition to getting good nutrition, this involves sleeping and taking vacations from exercise.

It is important to get a proper amount of quality sleep regularly. The amount of sleep needed varies among individuals. If you constantly need an alarm clock to get up in the morning, you are probably not getting enough sleep. If you are getting less than five hours a night, you may not be getting enough sleep. If you are getting more than ten hours a night, you may be getting too much sleep; if so, this may be a symptom of some abnormality and you should bring it to your physician's attention.

If the quality of your sleep is not what it should be, there are steps that can often be taken to improve it. The first step is to have a good place to sleep. This means a good, firm mattress or mattress and bedsprings. A high quality mattress on the floor or on an elevated piece of plywood is better than

109

a low quality mattress on a low quality set of bedsprings. Your room should be quiet, dark, and not too hot. If neighborhood noises disturb you, insulate your bedroom better or move to a quieter neighborhood. (If your children disturb you during the night, send them to an orphanage!) If your room is not dark enough, try taping aluminum foil on the insides of your bedroom windows. If your room is too warm in the summertime, buy a small, high-efficiency room air conditioner. If you have a good place to sleep and still don't sleep well, there are other factors to consider.

Are you getting enough exercise? If not, your body may be too full of energy to permit you to sleep. Get some regular, moderate exercise. On the other hand, it is possible that you are getting too much exercise. If so, cut back. This is especially true of competitive athletes. I have often been so banged up after a hockey game that it was almost impossible to sleep.

Are you troubled about your life? If you are under a great deal of temporary stress, you may not be able to sleep because you are worried about your problem. If so, perhaps steps can be taken to alleviate the problem. If not, read a good book until you get sleepy and don't worry about what you cannot control. As the Icelandic traditional poet wrote:

> Foolish is he who frets at night, and lies awake to
> worry:
> A weary man when morning comes, He finds all as bad
> as before.[35]

Sometimes one's sleeping partner is the cause of the problem. For example, if your partner snores or likes the room much cooler or warmer than you do, your sleep may be disturbed. If so, sleep in a different bedroom. Or change partners!

It is also important to sleep during regular hours. Someone who keeps a very irregular schedule may well have difficulty sleeping. The solution here is obvious: get on a regular schedule. If your job doesn't permit it, change jobs.

Napping can also interfere with getting a good night's sleep. If you nap regularly, make sure that you don't nap too long. If your naps exceed one hour in length, cut them back. If none of these suggestions works, see your physician.

It's an excellent idea to take vacations. If you are able to afford to travel away from your daily environment for a week or two or more every year, do so. Break your daily routine. We all tend to fall into the habit of living our daily lives without thinking much about what we are doing. Vacations can be a time for rethinking our daily habits.

I also suggest that you take breaks from your regular exercise program. It's good to get away from walking or running for a week or so each year. Switch to another exercise—or do nothing at all. Of course, if you stop exercising you'll immediately begin to lose all the benefits of exercising, but that's all right for a brief period of time. The psychological advantage of a switch or a temporary cessation will probably outweigh the physical disadvantages. I like to vacation, as I mentioned, in the bush. Often the water is too cold for swimming and there is no place to run (although paddling a canoe is excellent aerobic exercise). I find such vacations most refreshing and heartily recommend them.

111

6

Formal Education

Socrates was correct in believing that no one ever teaches anyone anything. Understanding is not something done to students; teachers do not give understanding to them. Rather, if it occurs at all, understanding is something students obtain themselves.[36] Learning is an activity that a student does. A teacher, like a book, is at best an aid for the student to use in educating himself. (Just as there are good [useful] and bad books, so there are good and bad teachers.) Socrates used the analogy of a midwife. Midwives were barren women who assisted other women in giving birth. Socrates said that his "art of midwifery is in general like theirs: the only difference is that my patients are men, not women, and my concern is not with the body but with the soul that is in travail of birth"; in other words, he assisted his students in their giving birth to understanding, in their development of wisdom.[37] Understanding, like giving birth to a baby, is difficult. One might think of teachers as like, say, the coaches of world-class figure skaters. It is possible to give birth to a baby without a midwife, but it is impossible to become a champion figure skater without a good coach. Yet coaches do not win championships. They simply try to bring the best out of their pupils.

They spend years encouraging their pupils to be the best possible skaters. It is like that with good teachers. Though only an aid, a teacher is an important aid.

There are, of course, other factors. For example, it helps if you happen to have parents who value a good education. It helps if you live in a society that values a good education. It helps if you are healthy enough to pursue your education energetically. It is obviously important that you have sufficient leisure to pursue your education; anyone who spends, for example, 14 hours a day in a rice paddy has little time for formal education. And so on. Nevertheless, for an adult, the chief responsibility for your formal education is yours.

Socrates was also correct in believing in the value of education.[38] I am convinced that one of the best ways to make consistently good decisions is to try deliberately to make decisions that you will not later regret. What is more regrettable than wasted potential? For this reason alone, everyone should get as much formal education as possible. (This recommendation should be slightly limited—see below.) Furthermore, persons with more formal education are quite likely to make much more money over the course of their lives than persons with less formal education.

It is important to take a moment to recognize the context of this discussion of formal education. The public elementary and high schools in this country are, in general, in poor shape. A century or so ago everyone admitted that the very best public schools in the world were found in the United States and Britain. That is not true today. A chief reason for this is that the very best persons are not becoming teachers. The education departments of our colleges tend to attract only mediocre students and they therefore tend to produce mediocre teachers. Why? We don't value teachers very highly. Being a teacher seems barely better than being a secretary. We certainly don't pay teachers very much. A business executive or a movie star or a professional athlete may make ten or twenty times as much money per year as a teacher. Public school teachers are also hamstrung by all sorts of rules that govern their art in the classroom. It is not surprising, then, that we don't have the best teachers—and how could we have the best schools without having the best teachers? And how could we have the best schools without having the best administrators? School administrators must answer to school boards— and the only qualification for being a member of a school board is getting more votes than one's opponent. So, however dedicated and popular school board members are, there is nothing to preclude their being ignorant or unintelligent. Mark Twain is once supposed to have remarked that school boards were "what God made after he practiced making idiots."

Since most persons in this country attend public schools, chances are that you have been cheated. You probably did not have the best teachers and the best books. Your school probably did not have an atmosphere conducive to learning. In high school you probably did not get four years of English, at least three years of some other important language, at least three years of mathematics, at least two years of history, and at least two years of science. Even if you had the courses, it is unlikely that they were rigorous enough. The difference between public and good private high schools on this score is quite remarkable. But if you were cheated, you are in good company.

Did you ever repaint a room? If so, you know that you cannot do a better job than the person who initially painted the room. One simply paints over the old paint—even if there is old paint in places where it shouldn't be.

It's a bit like that at the college level. A college professor must try to build on what has gone before. If what has gone before is not very good, a professor is very limited in what he is able to do because even the students who are motivated to try hard will lack the necessary background. Professors find themselves trying to teach students who lack the requisite intellectual skills such as reading and writing—skills they should have developed at (or before) the high school level. So there is a progression of decay. Poor elementary schools lead to poor high schools. Poor high schools lead to poor colleges. Poor colleges lead to poor graduate and professional schools. My discussion of formal education is grounded upon the recognition of this decay.

My purpose is not to develop a philosophy of education or even to suggest ways to improve our schools. It is rather to look at formal education from the point of view of the individual student in order to make some practical suggestions for getting as much out of the current system as possible.[39]

I have three suggestions concerning formal education.

1. Set appropriate goals.
2. Get as much appropriate formal education as possible.
3. Get as much as possible out of each course.

1. *Set appropriate goals.* If you do not have a high school diploma, why not get one? You may even be able to obtain one by passing a high school equivalency examination. Inquire at your local public high school for guidance.

Anyone capable of understanding this book is intellectually capable of attaining a bachelor's degree. There are three features necessary for a student to be successful: ability, background, and motivation. If you are reading this with comprehension, it is extremely likely that you have the ability. A more precise estimate of your ability could be obtained by taking the ACT or SAT examinations; your local high school college guidance counselor can help you obtain the necessary information. If your educational background is deficient, you have the ability to correct it. So the crucial factor is motivation. Why should anyone who has the ability to get a college education do so?

There are (at least) four different conceptions of the chief purpose of an undergraduate education. Let me briefly consider and evaluate each in turn.

The *classical* conception of education comes from such ancient thinkers as Plato and Aristotle. They argued that the purpose of education is to assist the student in living the best possible life. The most perfect human life was thought to be one that exercised the most perfect human faculty. Since the most perfect human faculty is that of reason, the best possible life would be the life of reason. Their ideal human being was a philosopher. (The Greeks did not mean by 'philosopher' what we mean by 'professional philosopher' or 'philosophy professor'.) Only philosophers were thought to be capable of knowing that which is fully real and, hence, only philosophers were thought to be able to make decisions based on knowledge of what is good (as opposed to making decisions based on mere opinion or emotion or chance).

There are two major problems with this view. First, many people lack the intellectual capacity to be philosophers. So this view is elitist in the sense that it simply excludes many, perhaps most, people from the best kind of life. (This was one reason for the historical emergence of Christianity, which is not elitist. After all, anyone who has faith may enter the Kingdom of God.) Second, this view is based on the claim that there is knowledge about the good. If this is false, then there is nothing special about the good for the philosopher to know. But if, as I believe, there is knowledge about the good, then this view is attractive.

The *utilitarian* conception of education comes from such early modern thinkers as Valla, Machiavelli, and Hobbes. They argued that the purpose of education is to assist the student in developing the power to pursue other ends; in other words, education is a means to the development of capacities that are in turn means to other ends. The best current example is that of an undergraduate as a future businessman. An undergraduate may major in finance or accounting or management in order to develop abilities that will make him more marketable in the job market. Studying accounting, then, is not an end in itself; it is a means to a further end, namely, a job as an accountant. The job is not an end either; it is merely a means to make money. Nor is money an end; it is valuable only as a means to other ends such as food or housing or political power. On this view, then, education is merely a means to something else.

There are three major problems with this view. First, it lacks flexibility. Knowing how to be an accountant is useless, for example, if there are no accounting jobs. This lack of flexibility could only be overcome by a broadly based education, which is exactly what the utilitarian conception does not propose. Second, and more important, any correct conception of education ought to acknowledge the intrinsic value of education. Even if it happens to have no practical effects, knowledge is itself an abstract good. Third, this conception of education as a means to something else rests on the assumption that the end, the something else, is already known. But what exactly is the end? What should our goals be? What, really, is the point of gaining various abilities? The attempt to answer this question should be part of what education is all about. For example, it is simply false that the point of life is to acquire as much money as possible. If so, why spend life making money?

The *professional* conception of education originally also comes from such ancient thinkers as Plato. In effect, he describes a professional training school in his *Republic*. The chief idea here is that the purpose of an undergraduate education is to train students to go on to graduate or professional schools. A student wanting to attend medical school, for example, ought to study chemistry and biology as an undergraduate. A student interested in becoming a scholar ought to study languages as an undergraduate. An undergraduate course of study ought to be a pre-graduate or pre-professional course of study. So the professional conception of education is the conception of education as pre-professional training.

As the educational apparatus is currently constituted, a student interested in going to medical school would doubtless be wise to be a 'pre-med' major. But this is only a practical consideration; I am here discussing the ideals of undergraduate education. The chief objection to this view is that there

119

is a difference between education and training. Education is not merely training—whether pre-professional or not. There is no theoretical reason why graduate and professional schools should be even located at undergraduate colleges. It is, of course, true that our undergraduate colleges serve as training grounds for graduate and professional schools for some students. But this should not be their chief function. Their chief function should be education—not merely training. In other words, there is again a confusion between means and ends. One may study biology, for example, as a means to some other end (for example, certification as a medical doctor) or as an end in itself (to understand living organisms). A student who studies it as a means is attempting to train himself; a student who studies it as an end is attempting to educate himself. Insofar as this difference is important, the professional conception of education should be rejected. Insofar as the two are compatible, there is no problem with combining them.

The *aesthetic* conception of education comes from those who reject the other conceptions. Anyone who holds this view objects to the classical conception, not on the basis of its elitism, but because of its supposedly mistaken view that there is knowledge of what is good. Anyone who holds this view objects to the utilitarian view because usefulness is not itself a virtue. The same for the professional conception. What is left? According to the aesthetic conception of education the purpose of an undergraduate education is to assist the student in the development of good taste. The chief idea here is that the difference between someone who is educated and someone who isn't is that only the former will have a developed aesthetic sensibility. Someone with a developed aesthetic

120

sensibility will know the difference between good and bad music, good and bad literature, good and bad painting, good and bad dance, good and bad drama, and so on. In this sense, an educated person will be a cultured person.

What is right about this view is the value that it places on art: art is valuable. Aesthetic appreciation is good. Beauty is an abstract good. But it is neither the only good nor the greatest good. What is wrong with this view is that it elevates uselessness to the level of being a virtue. Is education to have nothing to do with living life well? The ideal of art for the sake of art is empty. *Pace* James Joyce, by becoming artists (or art critics) we do not become gods. The ancient Greeks would have been astonished at this view. Thucydides, for example, expressly wrote his great history of the Peloponnesian War because he hoped that it would be useful: "It will be enough for me . . . if these words of mine are judged useful . . ."[40] The best reason to study history is to learn from it, to try to avoid the mistakes and to emulate the successes of others. This is not to deny that the study of history, like the study of art, can be rewarding in and of itself; it is to urge that such activities also be viewed as useful activities. Put it this way: what is the real difference between good and bad art? Isn't it that one is more useful to us than the other?

I suggest that the correct conception of education is what I have called the classical conception. It is, in a sense, elitist. But are not some lives better than other lives? It is a view that presupposes the existence of knowledge of what is good. If this is false, then this view of education is incoherent. (I return to this topic in the last chapter.)

If so, the appropriate general goal of an undergraduate education should be to enable one to know what is good, to live life better, to learn how to make consistently better decisions. For this reason, anyone with the ability should try to obtain an undergraduate education. Since life is worth living, it is worth living well.

This means that it would be wise to select a college that is strong in the humanities—philosophy, history, and literature and the other arts. If you already know your other goals with respect to formal education (for example, getting into medical school or landing a job in business or making new friends or finding a lover), obviously these are also relevant in selecting a college.

If you have not already done so, during your first two years, I suggest the following procedure for selecting courses. *i.* Any decent college will have certain distribution requirements. Satisfy these first. In other words, sample a variety of disciplines before settling down into just one. If you have never had a course in natural science, how can you rationally eliminate biology or geology or physics as a long term interest? It is reasonable to look around before committing yourself to a major field of study, which is a chief reason (in addition to trying to ensure that their undergraduates receive a broadly based education) why colleges have developed distribution requirements. *ii.* The professor is more important than the course. A good professor can bring to life what would otherwise seem an uninteresting subject. A bad professor can undermine your initial interest in even the most exciting subject. Every college has its 'star' professors. Find out who they are and take their introductory courses. You owe it to yourself.

2. *Get as much appropriate formal education as possible.* Anyone capable of comprehending this book has the intellectual ability to obtain a bachelor's degree at most colleges. If you don't yet have one, why not get one? The only important factor is motivation. If you have the ability and want it, you can get it. Don't let other considerations get in your way. And don't make excuses. You are never too old to learn. You are never too broke (or too rich) to learn. Find out what it takes to overcome such factors and overcome them.

If you have specific career goals, make an appropriate plan. For example, if you want to be a medical doctor, find out what it takes to get into medical school and plan your undergraduate curriculum accordingly. If you have no specific career goals, plan to major in one of the humanities; if you become enthused along the way about some other field, you can enter it. The best way to begin is simply to begin. Start taking courses. In all likelihood, you will find some discipline that you enjoy and are good at. If not, find a good academic advisor at your college and discuss your situation frankly with that person.

By the time that you satisfy the requirements for a bachelor's degree, you are likely to know whether or not you'll need additional formal education. If you need it, get it. The sooner that you get it, the easier it will be.

It is possible to get too much formal education. For example, if your goal is to become a concert pianist, it is neither necessary nor advisable to obtain a doctorate in music; at a certain point, what you must do is play the piano—not study about playing the piano. Another example is the 'professional' student. Some people so thoroughly enjoy being students, or so fear being nonstudents, that they tend to remain students for years. This phenomenon occurs at both the undergraduate

123

and graduate levels. Such persons are likely to develop many of the skills necessary to being good students—and they become so comfortable with those skills that they hesitate to get on with their lives. Being a student means preparing one-self for something else—and at a certain point there comes a time to get on with it.

On the other hand, many skills first learned as a student should be used throughout life. For example, every student should learn how to read and evaluate works of literature, philosophy, history, and science. These habits should be exercised throughout life, regardless of your career. Reading good literature with discernment and appreciation, for example, is one of the joys of living. If you fail to develop this skill as an undergraduate you are in danger of leading a life that is less rich and full than it should be.

3. *Get as much as possible out of each course.* Before making specific suggestions about doing well in courses, let me make two general suggestions.

First, set an appropriate goal for yourself for each course and work hard to satisfy it. I even recommend writing down this goal during the first week of the course. In general, there will be two sorts of goals that are appropriate; these depend upon the relation of the specific course to your overall plan. Either the course will fall within your major field of study or it will not. For example, let us suppose that you are an English major. *a.* Certain courses will be required or recommended as beneficial to your study of English, for example, a course in the works of Shakespeare. Your appropriate goal will be to obtain a rather sophisticated appreciation of Shakespeare's genius. *b.* Other courses that you will take will not directly relate to your major field of study. For example, as part of your satisfaction of your college's distribution requirements, you may find yourself in a geology course. You will obviously not approach its subject matter as a geology major would. Your appropriate goal should be to answer the question, 'Why would any sane person become a geologist?' After all, you may initially think, who would want to spend his life studying rocks? How boring! But not all geologists are insane; hence, there must be something interesting about rocks—otherwise there would not be any geologists. So you should think of your task in your introductory geology course as finding out what motivates someone to be a geologist. Once you find out, you are in a position to decide whether or not to pursue your study of geology. Even if you decide not to pursue it, you have for the first time made an informed decision about geology.

Educating yourself involves deciding to submit to certain standards. By choosing a college, you have chosen that college's standards. To succeed, you had to satisfy its distribution requirements and found yourself in a geology course. After you have determined for yourself whether or not geology is interesting enough for you to pursue further, you have satisfied one of the college's distribution requirements. You should have also satisfied one of your own standards. After all, why go through life not understanding what motivates some people to be geologists? So, set a goal for each course that is appropriate for you and work hard to satisfy it.

Second, think of yourself as an excellent student and act accordingly. Many students seem to think of themselves as average students and seem perfectly satisfied with average work. But if you are going to be a student at all, why not be an excellent one? Why do a job poorly? Suppose, for example, that your professor has given you a reading assignment and that you have read the material once. Ask yourself: Would an excellent student read this material only once or would he read it and reread it until he has mastered it? If he would do the latter, you should go back to work. Or suppose that you have been doing research for a paper and wonder if you have done enough. Ask yourself: Would an excellent student do more research on this topic than I have now done? If so, spend some more time in the library. Or suppose that you are preparing for an examination. Ask yourself: Would an excellent student have studied more for this exam than I now have? If so, review the material for a while longer. It is true that not every student has the time or the ability to be an excellent student. But it is also true that nearly every student has the time and the ability, through harder work, to become a better student.

Notice that, with respect to these two general suggestions, I have mentioned setting and satisfying your own goals. Work to master the subject matter enough to satisfy yourself. Do not simply work to master the subject matter enough to satisfy your professor. Your professor's standards may not be ones that are appropriate for you in your circumstances. Your professor is merely an aid for you to use in educating yourself. It is perfectly possible for you to satisfy your professor's standards but not your own—and vice-versa. Ultimately, it is your own assessment of your work that counts—not your professor's.

On the other hand, your professor is supposed to understand the subject matter better than you do and, if you are doing most of the work anyway, there is nothing wrong with trying to obtain from him a high evaluation. Permit me some specific tips for doing better in courses.

126

In Class: Attend every class. There is no substitute for attendance.

Take good notes during class. There are two ways to take notes. By experimentation, determine which way works better for you. *i.* Do not try to write down everything your professor says. Try to understand what he says as he goes along and try to jot down the main points. *ii.* Try to write down as much as possible of what the professor says. Don't worry about understanding everything the first time that you hear it; you can develop your understanding later as you read and think about your notes. Whichever of these methods you use, form the habit of reviewing your notes later the same day that they were taken. Try to recreate what your professor said. A daily five minute review is likely to increase greatly your retention of the material.

Reading Assignments: Force yourself to read actively instead of passively. A good method is the SQ3R method: survey, question, read, recite, review. Survey the passage to be read in order to orient your thinking. Raise questions before you read it, while you are reading it, and after you have read it. After you finish reading it, close the book and recite to yourself the chief ideas or main arguments of the passage. Review the passage to ensure that you have understood it correctly. You may need to reread the passage once or twice to ensure mastery of it. If you cannot understand it, try it again the next day. If something remains unclear, raise a question about it in class. Perhaps it makes no sense to you because it is senseless; this certainly happens occasionally in philosophy.

Exams: The real value of an exam is in the preparation— so don't skip it. Find out as early as possible the kind of exam you will be taking. Suppose, for example, that you find out the first day of class that the midterm exam will be a short answer essay test that will be based primarily on material covered in class. Anticipate the questions that could be asked. As the weeks go by, make a list of those questions and answer them. Just before the exam, review those questions and answers to make sure that you remember them. Review, also, your class notes and the reading assignments. If you force yourself to develop good study habits, preparing for exams will be easy since you'll be doing it continuously. And get a good night's sleep the night before an exam.

When taking an exam, read all the questions and instructions first. Ask your professor to explain any unclear questions. Answer the questions to which you know the answers before attempting to answer the other questions. Budget your time. Do not, for example, spend half your time on an answer that is worth only 20 percent of your score (unless, of course, you know that you have answered all the other questions correctly). Bring a watch to the exam—and an extra pen. Remember that you will be graded not on what you know, but on what you write down. So assume that your professor knows nothing; write down everything that is relevant to your answer. Try to write, not just so that you can be understood, but so that you cannot be misunderstood. Do not waste either your own time or your professor's by writing what is irrelevant to the question. Be sure to answer every part of every question.

When the exam is returned, check your professor's arithmetic. Find out exactly where you erred. Learn from your mistakes. Identify your weaknesses and correct them before the next exam. Never fail twice for the same reason.

Papers: Write on the assigned topic if your professor

assigns one. If your professor lets you select your own topic, make a tentative choice by choosing one that is limited but challenging, and get your professor's approval and advice before doing much work on it (even if his approval is not required). The simple step of securing his approval and soliciting his advice may save you fruitless hours of hard work.

If your professor gives you a certain format to follow, follow it exactly. If not, use some standard guide (for example, the latest edition of *The MLA Style Sheet*) for writing foot-notes and bibliography. Work hard to ensure that your paper has a good physical appearance. It should be neat, clean, and legible. For example, if your typewriter needs cleaning, clean it. If its ribbon is worn, replace it. Type it or print it on stout (at least twenty pound), standard size (8" by 11"), white bond paper. Submit the original—not a copy. Remember that your professor will be impressed, one way or the other, by the appearance of your paper. And always keep a copy in case your professor loses your paper.

A good paper is well-organized. It ought to contain a beginning, a middle, and an end. Suppose that you are writing a short paper. It should contain an introductory paragraph. The purpose of this paragraph is to focus your reader's attention on your chief conclusion, your thesis. Therefore, this paragraph should contain, normally as its last sentence, a statement of your thesis. (You are not writing a detective story; you should not spring your thesis on the unwary reader at the end.) In the body of the paper you should give the reasons for accepting your thesis. It is usually a good technique to raise and answer significant objections to your thesis. The conclusion of your paper should restate your thesis and put it in perspective.

Your goal is to write a clear, coherent paper. The following questions may be useful. Does my paper have a beginning, middle, and end? Will my reader know at all times where he is? What is my thesis? Is it clearly stated? Are any auxiliary theses clearly stated? Are important concepts explained? Are examples used to explain important concepts? If so, are the examples appropriate and helpful? Are there any better ones? Are technical terms, if any, clearly defined? Are any analogies used? If so, are they appropriate and helpful? Are there any better ones? What are the reasons given for accepting the thesis? Are the chief arguments clearly stated? Is the reasoning good? Are the claims made in the paper consistent with one another? Are obvious or significant objections raised and answered? Are apparent counterexamples considered? Are fundamental assumptions clearly stated? Are important issues raised by the conclusion? Are these issues noted? Is the conclusion overstated or is it put into the proper perspective?

Proofread your paper carefully. Always have someone else proofread it too. (Perhaps you can return the favor.) Make the necessary corrections neatly.

Submit your paper on time. In general, avoid asking your professors for special treatment. Impress them with your hard work and dependability.

There are two other permanent benefits to completing your formal education that I wish to mention in conclusion. Just as with quitting smoking or permanently improving your dietary or exercise habits, completing your formal education will increase your self-esteem. Self-esteem is a good. Graduating is an important accomplishment and you should feel good about it. It should give you a permanent morale boost: you have struggled hard for a long time toward a valuable

130

goal—and succeeded! Congratulate yourself! Feel good about being you!

And graduating will also improve the way that others evaluate you. Once they know, their opinion of you will permanently improve. Even if they do not particularly value a college education, they will admire you for setting and achieving a long-term objective. Because your credentials have been permanently improved, opportunities will be available to you that would not have been available otherwise. This is particularly true with respect to earning money.

7

Working

Most adult human beings spend most of their waking hours either working, preparing for work, or recovering from work. In our society the typical compensation for this effort is money from wages, salaries, or commissions; the immediate goal of working is to obtain money. In our society most persons work for companies (whether partnerships or corporations). Working for a company is having a job. This chapter is about having a job.

A job may be one that contributes to one's Project or one that does not. As an example of the former, suppose that Alex's major Project, the activity that contributes most to the meaning of his life, is to work to preserve our natural resources (for example, our forests, our wildlife, and so on), and that Alex secures a position as an executive of an environmental organization such as the National Audubon Society or the Natural Resources Defense Council. Alex is lucky: he is compensated for his work by more than just money. The test of the difference between the two sorts of jobs is whether you would do the work even if you would receive a paycheck regardless of whether or not you did the work. If so, it is a job that contributes to your Project (or to one of your Projects); if not, it isn't. As an example of the latter, suppose that Betty has a job in a glass factory that manufactures windshields for automobiles and trucks. Betty does not like spending the best hours of her life in a glass factory, but her hourly wage is good and she needs the money. She is obviously not as lucky as Alex.

I would guess that most working people have jobs that do not contribute to their Projects. (Most working people may not even have Projects.) A job that contributes to your Project(s) is better than one that doesn't; it is better to work at your own Project(s) than not to work at them. The problem for most working people is how to shift from working at jobs that do not contribute to their Projects to working at tasks that contribute to their Projects. My solution to this problem is presented in this chapter and the next. My primary topic in this chapter is how to make the best of your job even if it doesn't contribute to your Project(s).

There are many features of a job that are irrelevant to this topic. One might examine the goods or services produced by the job, their effect upon both workers and consumers, the effects of the manufacturing processes (if any) on workers, consumers, and the environment, and so on. Though these are interesting subjects, I do not discuss them.

From the point of view of a worker's Project(s), a job often becomes a dead-end. Many people seem to complete their formal education, land a job, and get stuck right there until retirement. Inertia sets in. Human beings have a truly astounding capacity to adjust to unfavorable circumstances. Suppose that Betty, for example, though she hates her job, develops secondary satisfactions while working in the glass factory. She makes friends with several of her co-workers; she commutes to work with them, spends time with them away from work, and together they volunteer their services to some charitable organization thereby deriving some lasting satisfaction. Suppose, furthermore, that she gets married and she and her husband raise and educate two children. These secondary Projects serve to generate enough meaning in her life for her to endure her long years at the glass factory.

But consider an alternative. Surely it would be better for Betty if she could afford not to work at the glass factory. She could then elevate her friendships, volunteer work, and family life from secondary to primary status. Or she could adopt a new Project such as becoming a physician or an archaeologist. And if she became independently wealthy, she would be able to devote many more hours to helping people through her charitable work. She could, in other words, do with her life what she really wanted. She could work full-time at her own Projects instead of at the glass factory.

I feel much compassion for people such as Betty. A better world could be had if we could somehow organize life in such a way that people could do what they most wanted to do. The current world is one in which economic necessity forces many people to spend most of their waking lives doing what they do not really want to do. As Marx put it in *The German Ideology*, "as soon as the division of labour comes into being, each man has a particular, exclusive sphere of activity, which is forced upon him and from which he cannot escape. He is a hunter, a fisherman, a shepherd, or a critical critic, and must remain so if he does not want to lose his means of livelihood".[41] Betty, for example, needs money to live. Where would she get it if she were to quit her job at the glass factory to pursue key Projects? The alternative is to create a society in which people are really free to do what they want (within, of course, legal and moral limits). Marx urges us to imagine a society "where nobody has one exclusive sphere of activity but each can become accomplished in any branch he wishes." In such a society, it would be possible "for me to do one thing today and another tomorrow, to hunt in the morning, fish in the afternoon, rear cattle in the evening, criticize after dinner, just as I have a mind, without ever becoming hunter, fisherman, shepherd or critic." Since we have created the present economic and social organization that enslaves people like Betty, we can (and should) change it.

Consideration of such general change is beyond the scope of this book. I want to point out, however, that the good life that Marx sketches is available here and now. It is, unfortunately, not available for everyone. But it is at least available in our society for every individual of at least 'tolerable' abilities who works at it effectively.

The accumulation of money is a Project unworthy of a human being. Making money is not the meaning of life. The most ambitious capitalists may understand that the mere accumulation of money is not an end in itself. By itself, a building full of money is just a building full of pieces of paper or metal. Money is a means to an end. The end is the good life. And, although money is doubtless useful in attaining the good life, we should have the same attitude toward money as that of the ancient Japanese samurai: we should never think about it. It isn't worth thinking about. Think instead about that which is valuable in itself.

The only way to attain this attitude is to have enough money to pursue your Projects full-time. Otherwise, you will be forced to think about it. But how should you obtain enough money?

It is not merely by having a job. Otherwise, everyone with a job would have enough money, which they obviously don't.

It is by accumulating a personal endowment that is sufficiently large that you can live off the earnings of the endowment. Creation of such an endowment is the topic of the next chapter. A prior step in creating an endowment is getting a job. A job allows you to secure your credit rating, and a good credit rating can be turned into an endowment. The purpose of securing steady employment, therefore, should be to get rid of the need for steady employment. A job is merely a step on the way to becoming independently wealthy. Anyone who is independently wealthy does not need a job. It is only the independently wealthy who can afford to adopt the samurai's attitude toward money.

This should complement my remarks in Chapter 6 about formal education. If you were to educate yourself with only a view toward getting a job you would be wasting your formal education. What counts in life are goods that are intrinsically valuable. Working at your Project is intrinsically valuable. Merely working at a job that does not contribute to your Project is a waste of your life. What is worse than a wasted life? People like Betty should use their present situations as stepping stones to better situations; in other words, use your job to get rid of it.

Trying to become wealthy without having a job is impractical and is not a reasonable expectation for most people. On the path to fiscal well-being, therefore, it is best to think of having a job as the necessary second step that follows the first step of completing one's formal education. A diploma is often a necessary condition of obtaining a well-paying job.

Human needs are features of life whose satisfaction is a necessary condition of human well-being. Humans have needs, for example, for a good diet, for exercise and for emotional security. Needs may be 'felt' or 'unfelt'. Suppose, for example, that I were to become feverishly ill for a week or two. Because it is unwise to exercise with a fever, I would not exercise for that time. Since I am accustomed to regular exercise, I would actually feel the need for exercise. I would feel myself degenerating more rapidly than usual and I would not feel physically well until I recovered from my illness and began exercising again. On the other hand, suppose that Peter is unaccustomed to regular exercise and, so, unaccustomed to feeling good physically. He may or may not be ignorant of the benefits of regular exercise, but he simply would fail to experience a need for it. My need for exercise is a felt need; Peter's need for exercise is an unfelt need. Consider a different example. Suppose that we were to discover a tribe of humans who live on the edge of subsistence and that a physician who examined them found the whole tribe to be suffering from a specific nutritional deficiency. Because they had never experienced a proper diet, none of them would experience a felt need for the missing nutrient.

This distinction has economic importance because people purchase goods only when they experience a need for them. People do not always purchase items that are good for them. Junk food is not good for people, but people purchase it because they feel a need for it. Companies make money by producing and marketing goods that people feel a need to purchase. Companies exist to make money; a good company will make money in a legally and morally acceptable way.

Try to land a job at a good company that is making money. You want secure employment to establish credit, and employment at a good company that is making money is likely to provide more security than employment elsewhere.

It does not particularly matter whether you do physical ('blue collar') or intellectual ('white collar') labor. Each has advantages and disadvantages, and you can teach yourself to compensate for the relevant disadvantages. If you do physical labor, for example, you will be better off doing your exercise in the morning before work because you are likely to be too tired later to exercise. On the other hand, if you do intellectual labor you may be better off doing your exercise after work because your job may be more stressful, and exercise after work will tend to alleviate the day's burden of stress.

Choose a job that will not be too debilitating. The shift you work is irrelevant, for example, because after about two weeks your body will adjust physiologically to the shift.[42] A job that constantly rotates shifts, however, is too debilitating; policemen, firemen, nurses, and others who find themselves in this position complain, with good reason, of never feeling rested.

Other things being equal, a job that pays more is obviously better than a job that pays less. But there is a trade-off: a job that pays only moderately is better than a job that is debilitating and pays well. You should keep in mind the point of a job: it is to provide for your needs and to establish credit. This is possible even if you do not make a lot of money. It is not the job that will create your fortune; it is what you do outside the workplace (see Chapter 8). Take a job, therefore, that is not too debilitating, not too draining.

Select and try to secure the sort of job that you would like

139

to work at temporarily. Keep your expectations modest: your purpose is to secure regular employment—not to be hired as company president.

Don't believe everything that you may have heard about job training. If you have the confidence bred by a broadly-based educational background there are very few jobs that you cannot quickly learn how to do well. You don't need to have graduated from a prestigious journalism school to become an excellent journalist. You don't need an M.B.A. from Harvard to become an excellent manager. You don't even need to have a B.S. in engineering, much less be a Professional Engineer, to land an engineering job. One of my brothers, for example, was a history major at college. Before he even graduated, he was hired by a company who recognized his potential and trained him as an engineer. In less than a year the company sent him out on his own and, in an engineering position, he spent a number of years in the U.S.S.R. and East Germany amassing a small fortune. This company's policy was not to hire young persons who had been trained as engineers since such persons thought they knew everything and were very hard to train; the company preferred young persons with potential who were perfectly willing to be trained to do things exactly as the company wanted them done.

Such stories are not as uncommon as one might think. Robert Townsend, for example, took over the Avis Rent-a-Car Company. It had been in the red for the 13 years of its existence. Three years after he took it over, it made nine million dollars. Townsend puts it quite simply: "The only way I know to get somebody trained is on the job."[43] My impression is that many good executives have learned the same thing. I had a relative who owned three construction companies and ran two of them. He told me that only about one-third of his time was spent on construction concerns; the other two-thirds was spent in communication, in other words, dealing with customers and employees. A good manager is a communicator. Good communicators understand people. I know of no better way to understand people than by experiencing them directly over the years and by experiencing them indirectly through the study of literature, history, philosophy and science. My wife, for example, majored in college in English and philosophy. She took a job with a company that manufactures architecturally engineered window products for commercial and industrial buildings. She largely taught herself the job, with the company helping by paying for her enrollment in courses on how to read blueprints and on how to sell more effectively. In her second year she was made sales manager of the company, largely because she is an excellent communicator. The point is not to be afraid to request an interview for a job that you want even if you lack some formal training. You won't get a job as a surgeon, but you might land a much better job than you initially thought possible.

I have three suggestions for obtaining and keeping a job.

1. Don't lie.
2. Train yourself to be successful.
3. Make every decision as if you owned the company.

1. *Don't lie.* Townsend is right when he says: *"Don't con anybody.* Not your wife. Not your children. Not your employees. Not your customers. Not your stockholders. Not your boss. Not your associates. Not your suppliers. Not your regulatory authorities. Not even your competitors. *Don't con yourself either.*[44]

Lying is not only immoral, it is bad policy. From the moment that you begin to apply for the job until the moment that you leave it, never say what is untrue. The reasons are obvious.

But this maxim is in need of qualification: sometimes it is better to say nothing than to speak the truth. For example, suppose that you have begun a new job, that your initial impression of your boss is that he is incompetent, and that some fellow employee asks you what you think of your boss. In truth, you think that he is incompetent, but it does no good to say it. Keep your own counsel. Nobody is entitled to your opinion about this. You need not lie, either. Just avoid answering. An honest answer here could cost you your job (if, say, your fellow employee mentions your opinion to your boss and your boss then starts looking for some reason to fire you). Honesty is not a license for tactlessness. And, of course, your initial impression of your boss may be incorrect.

There is no good reason to lie. Suppose that you don't have the training that you think will be required for the job; don't lie on the application form. If they check it out, you'll become known both as a liar and as under-qualified. The same goes for the interview. If you have done your homework, you know what the company does and how well they are doing. You know what assets you would be able to bring to the company. You have dressed appropriately for the interview and are on time and well rested. You have thought about what sorts of questions you may be asked—and their answers (which is exactly like any good student before an exam or the President before a news conference). But there is no point in being nervous. Just relax and be yourself. If you were interviewing someone for a job to become your co-worker, what would you look for? Certainly you would look for the appropriate credentials, but that search would be modified by your knowledge that whoever you hire will only be able to master the job by on-the-job training. You would almost certainly look for someone you like. After all, you might well be spending many hours with this person and it is very important that you get along well. Suppose that you were interviewing persons for a job and Fred comes in to be interviewed. If you love baseball and Fred doesn't even know that the New York Yankees are a baseball team, if you care about the quality of the environment and Fred couldn't care less about pollution, if you are a family man and Fred is a swinging bachelor, if you love to read and Fred never cracks a book, would you really hire Fred even if he were well-qualified? What would you talk about during lunch? Likability is the most important asset in securing a job. Anyone who has self-confidence (self-esteem, a sense of self-worth) is more likely to be open to and liked by others than someone who lacks self-confidence. Someone who is in control is more likely to be self-confident than someone who isn't. Are you in control? Have you, for example, eliminated your bad physical habits? Have you developed good physical habits? Have you achieved a broadly-based formal education? If so, you will be more likely to relate to the interviewer on a warm, human level. Chances are that you'll have something in common to build upon. If so, the interviewer is more likely to like you and, so, more likely to hire you. So relax, smile, and let your hard work at self-improvement pay off.

2. *Train yourself to be successful.* Think of what a successful employee would do. And then do it.

For example, consider how you dress for work. If you are a drill press operator, your clothing may make little difference, but for many jobs the way that you dress makes an important, but often neglected, impression on the people you meet professionally or socially. If you doubt this, try the following experiment. If you are a man, wear a three-piece suit with appropriate shirt and tie the next time that you go shopping. The time after that, wear a black leather motorcycle jacket, blue jeans, and engineer boots. My experience has been that clerks will almost always give you much better service if you are wearing a suit.

Just as it is possible to exercise for different people (as the illustration in Chapter 5 from Bill Bradley shows), so it is possible to dress for different people. You can dress for yourself. You can dress for your spouse. You can dress for your parents. You can dress for your boss. And so on. For whom should you dress?

When you are on the job it is best to dress for success on the job. What exactly is dressing for success on the job? The answer is indicated by empirical research. John T. Molloy has done some research on this and his general answer is that "in matters of clothing, conservative, class-conscious conformity is absolutely essential to the individual success of the American business and professional man".[45] Clothing has little effect on the wearer. But it greatly effects those with whom the wearer comes in contact. So if you have a job that brings you into contact with people and if you wish to be successful, wear clothing that will have a positive effect on the people that you meet. Which clothing has a positive effect? Read the research,

144

such as Molloy's, and find out. You'll discover some rather simple rules that you can apply to your own case by learning which materials and colors and patterns of suits should be matched to your physique and skin coloring and age and by learning that what looks appropriate in New York City may not look appropriate in San Francisco or Houston. You can train yourself to be more successful on the job by training yourself to dress for success.

This is possible in other areas as well. If you have a weak, ineffective voice, you can retrain your voice so that you speak in a more pleasing, more natural way. Only a fool thinks that the end of his formal education is the end of his education.

Most jobs have a human and a nonhuman component, and you should work at being successful at each. With respect to working with nonhuman tools, machines, and products, try to master them thoroughly. Try to know more about the product you are selling than anyone else ever has. Try to be better at that computer terminal than anyone else ever has. It may take years of practice, but why not be the best? And, once you are the best, don't be satisfied with your present skills: look around for more opportunities. Never let yourself become so complacent and self-satisfied that you are unwilling to challenge yourself, unwilling to grow. If you wind up in a rut, you should consider changing jobs to avoid the bad habit of switching off your brain when you are on the job. With respect to working with humans, the best way to be successful is to work to improve your own character (virtue, what Confucius called *jen*) so that your behavior will naturally reflect your inner goodness. When Confucius was asked for a maxim to be acted upon throughout life, he replied, "Surely the maxim of charity is such: 'Do not unto others what you

145

would not they should do unto you'",[46] which is the negative version of Christ's Golden Rule. It's a good maxim. For example, suppose that you find yourself in a position of leadership and you have to make an important decision. Why not consult with your staff and subordinates before making the decision? They'll appreciate being asked and they may give you some good advice. And, once you have decided, explain your reasons for your decision. Even those who would not have made the same decision will at least feel that you considered their advice even though you decided to override it for reasons that they can understand. Isn't that the kind of a leader you would want to follow? Or suppose that you are an employee with a suggestion for improving the company. And suppose that, fearing that your boss will try to take credit for your suggestion if you make it to him, you go over his head and make your suggestion to your boss's boss. But, if you were your boss, would you want an employee to go over your head with a suggestion? Hardly, so don't avoid the chain of command unless it is absolutely necessary. Besides, even if your boss were to take credit for your suggestion, so what? Won't the company be improved anyway? Isn't that the goal?

3. *Make every decision as if you owned the company.* This is really my most important suggestion. If you owned the company, would you want your employees to lie? Of course not. If you owned the company, would you want your employees to take the trouble to train themselves to be successful? Of course you would.

If you owned the company, you would try to make each decision for the good of the company. You might be mistaken about what actually was good for the company, but at least your motivation would be the right one in every instance.

146

What separates the best owners, then, from the others is not motivation but knowledge. A company does not exist in isolation; a company exists in a physical, social, and economic environment. What is good for a company does not exist in isolation, either; it exists in a context of physical, social, and economic goods. It is no easy matter to understand these goods and their relationships. The best owners, then, will tend to be the ones with a broadly-based educational background. The best employees will be the ones who are able to make decisions as if they were the best owners; they, too, will tend to be the ones with a broadly-based educational background. If so, this strengthens my recommendation in the last chapter about devoting your formal education to trying to obtain a broadly-based education.

If you have been organizing your physical habits so that they contribute to, instead of detracting from, your chances of success, you have already been making yourself into a better employee. If you owned the company, would you want your employees to quit smoking (and to eliminate their other detrimental physical habits)? Of course you would. Smoking greatly decreases the productivity of workers; smokers tend to miss more work due to illness than nonsmokers. Obviously, their health care costs are higher. If you owned the company, would you want your employees to eat a moderate, properly balanced diet? Of course you would. If you owned the company, would you want your employees to get a sufficient amount of regular, moderate exercise? Of course you would. So the physical improvements that I have already discussed are likely to make you a better employee.

Making decisions as if you owned the company is not the same as making decisions to please your boss. I have heard it said that the right way to get ahead in an organization is to determine what your boss wants and to do it. Maybe, maybe not. It depends on whether what your boss wants is in the best interests of the company. It's a bit analogous to the situation of a student's approach to being successful in a course. Every student has a choice in every course to work for himself or work for the professor. I previously suggested that a student should set his own goals and work to satisfy them. This is not necessarily the best way to become a straight A student— but it is the best way to become a successful student. If a student sets the appropriate goal for a course, has the ability to do well, has the motivation to work hard enough, and works hard enough, and, if the professor has the same goal and doesn't make any mistake in evaluating the student's performance, then, and only then, will the student do well according to the professor (in other words, receive a high grade). It may seem as if the chances of this happening are very slim, but my experience as both a student and a professor suggests that this happens more often than not. And if it doesn't happen, so what?

For whom should you live? Live for yourself. The alternative is to live for someone else, and the problem with this alternative is that that other person may not know what he is doing. If you know that another person knows what he is doing, it is only because you know what ought to be done; and, if you know what ought to be done, why not just do it? A student should work for himself; a student should not just work for his professor. If the student and the professor are doing their jobs well, the process will turn out well. Similarly, an employee should work for himself. He should not just work for his boss. If the employee is doing his job well and if his boss is doing his job well, the process will turn out well.

Unfortunately, the process does not always turn out well. The world is not necessarily just; life is unfair. Students who are evaluated unfairly can at least take solace in the fact that they satisfied themselves. Employees who are evaluated unfairly can at least take solace in the fact that they satisfied themselves.

In neither case do I ever recommend abandoning one's principles in an effort to get ahead. Never 'kiss ass'. If you don't, you may be amazed at how successful you become. I learned that lesson as an undergraduate taking a philosophy of language course. Then, as now, I thought that the so-called 'linguistic turn' was the wrong turn for contemporary philosophers to take. My professor obviously believed that it was the correct turn. My grade in the course depended entirely upon one term paper. I had the choice of writing either what I thought he wanted me to write or what I wanted to write about the philosophy of language. I thought 'to hell with him' and chose the latter. To my amazement I received an excellent grade; though my professor disagreed with me, he thought that my argument showed that I was trying to think things through for myself, which is probably what he wanted all along. One doesn't have to compromise one's principles to get ahead in business, either, according to Townsend. "The reason for this is that everybody else is so busy selling out, or has sold out so often, that when *you* come along and *don't* sell out or compromise, you stand out immediately"[47] I assume he means that you'll stand out positively and be marked for advancement. If it happens that you stand out negatively for not compromising your principles, get out of that company and find one worth working for.

There is waste in every organization. The wasted time and effort that you notice cannot be eliminated overnight. But, if you owned the company, would you want any waste in the organization? Of course not. Therefore, when you are on the job, eliminate whatever waste you are able to eliminate. It is not just the right way to act; somebody is probably noticing.

So even though your job may be nothing but a temporary inconvenience, as all our grandfathers used to say, if a job is worth doing, it is worth doing well.

8

Financial Independence

Suppose that your situation is the following. You have had a thorough physical examination and have used your physician's advice to improve your physical well-being by quitting smoking and eliminating your other bad physical habits. You have begun to eat a properly balanced, moderate amount of food. You have begun to get sufficient regular exercise. You have completed your formal education. And you are working successfully at a satisfactory job. What next?

It is written in the Gospel According to Saint Bradford: *Work to attain financial independence.* Financial independence is having enough money to do what you want without having a job. My gospel differs from other gospels in that everything in mine is eminently revisable in the light of your own experience and understanding. If you have a job that contributes to the success of your Project, you may not want to attain financial independence. Even if you retain your job, however, it's a good feeling not to have to have it. This chapter is about financial independence.

Each of us participates in an economic system that distributes goods and services. Different economic systems are possible. Ours is largely driven by the market. That is a matter of fact. The issue is how to attain financial independence under the present conditions. The issue concerning whether or not it ought to be driven by the market is not relevant to the discussion in this chapter.[48]

One of the glories of our society is that financial independence is available to any individual who has tolerable abilities and who is well-motivated. It does not come, however, without effort. (This, of course, is not true for those who inherit financial independence. But, believe it or not, there is a disadvantage to inheriting it: you will not have to teach yourself how to become financially independent. So, if you should lose your inheritance, you might be in the position of being broke and not knowing what to do about it. On the other hand, if you make yourself financially independent you will also have learned how to become financially independent. That knowledge contributes greatly to peace of mind—whether you are broke or not.) Do not be deceived about that. The effort required is in addition to that required to work at an ordinary job. On the other hand, if you are in control of your life you are likely to have the extra energy required. If you do not undermine your chances of success with bad physical habits; if you eat, rest, and exercise properly; if you limit the amount of time consumed by activities such as raising children or watching television, you are more likely to have the energy required to attain financial independence. Furthermore, as I discovered rather to my own amazement, becoming financially independent can actually be fun! You may come to enjoy it even more than your regular exercise. If you doubt this, work at it for six months.

It need not take more than 30 to 60 minutes of daily extra effort. Once you have it, you can, if you wish, spend all your time raising children or watching television.

The first step is to believe that it is possible. If you assume that attaining financial independence is impossible, you won't work to attain it. But many people have achieved it. Why shouldn't you?

It is crucial to formulate a plan for success. It is extremely unlikely that you will ever be financially independent unless you organize your efforts and work efficiently, over a period of years, to attain it.

Your plan should take into account the features of our present economic system. The key to success within that system is to *provide at a competitive price a product or service that satisfies a felt need.* That's easy to say and difficult to do. There are at least two reasons why it is difficult to come up with a plan for success.[49] First, at least in theory, except for taking risk and uncertainty into consideration, the rate of return on investment in all major categories of investment is the same. Everyone knows that the greater the risk, the greater the potential return. But if you are consi-dering two investments that have the same degree of risk and uncertainty there may be no greater return from one than from the other, there may be no purely economic reason to prefer one to the other. Second, if something has a market value, that value is the present value of the expected future income it will provide. For example, if you own an apartment building, its market value is the present value of the expected future income that that building will provide (and factors like tax breaks would be included). But the future may not continue to resemble the past; expected future income may not turn out to be actual future income. As Hume argued, we lack a clear under-standing of the concept of nondemonstrative evidence.[50]

153

The difficulty is that any plan that fails to be realistic, fails to consider the fundamental features of our economic system, will be unsatisfactory and that, even if one understands its present features, those features may not be the same in the future.

Your plan should also take into consideration your individual talents and circumstances. It is not as if a machine will somehow execute whatever plan you come up with: you must execute it. So I could not possibly provide such a personal plan in this chapter. Instead, I suggest certain general principles that may be of use to you and give specific examples of them.

The general principles I suggest are:

1. Create a financial reserve.
2. Create an investment fund.
3. Develop a plan for investing your investment fund.
4. Execute your plan.

1. *Create a financial reserve.* The sole purpose of your financial reserve is to prevent your going backwards financially. In other words, it is intended to get you through financial emergencies, unexpected expensive contingencies. Your reserve has two parts: a cash reserve and appropriate insurance.

Your cash reserve should not be less than three times your monthly mortgage or rent payment. If you are very conservative, double that. It should be money that is safe and quickly accessible; I suggest that you keep it in a passbook savings account at a bank. Once you have a sufficient amount in it, forget about it. If, on occasion, you need to dip into it, replen-

Appropriate insurance will at least be a sufficient amount of motor vehicle (if you drive), health, disability, and renter's or homeowner's insurance. It will probably also include an umbrella policy of at least one million dollars and a small term life insurance policy. If you own any other real property such as an apartment building it should also be covered. Some of this insurance may be provided by your employer, but the rest you'll have to buy from an insurance agent. Naturally, it's a good idea to shop around before purchasing. For example, *Consumer Reports* periodically evaluates the policies offered by national companies. On the theory that two heads are better than one, you may find it best to have two insurance agents working for you.

Where should you get the money for your cash reserve and your insurance policies? I suggest that you save it. When you are paying your bills each month, pay yourself first. Save at least five percent of your net income. Once you have filled your cash reserve and purchased your insurance policies, your habit of saving will help to build your investment fund.

Permit me some general remarks about the care and handling of money. The cash that you earn by working at your job is in short supply, so teach yourself not to waste it. For example, you should not be spending more than 25 percent of your gross income on your rent or mortgage payment. You should not be wasting money at the grocery store on highly processed foods; less processed foods are generally less expensive, as well as nutritionally more valuable. Nor should you be paying others routinely to do your cooking for you for the same reasons. Teach yourself the difference between (initial) price and (long term) cost: a pair of shoes that retails for $200 may be less expensive in the long run than a pair of $50 shoes. A good objective evaluation of goods on the marketplace is *Consumer Reports* magazine. I have subscribed for years, and each year I more than save the price of my subscription by buying more wisely. The next time that you are in the market for, say, an automobile or a refrigerator, why not give it a try? There should be a copy in your local public library.

Teach yourself a bit about money management. This will help you eliminate whatever screwy ideas about money you happen to have picked up. For example, forget about getting rich quick; you won't. (Even if you happened, say, to win a lottery, unless you knew how to manage money properly you'd likely lose it in a short time.) And forget the idea that someone else is responsible for your financial well-being; you are responsible. Notice that it is mostly poor people who gamble or who think that the government will take care of them. Poor people don't have the right ideas about money management; don't emulate them. Begin to think like a rich person.

That may not be as easy as it sounds. Often people believe that being in financial debt is bad. But this is false. If you never go into debt, it is extremely unlikely that you will ever be financially independent. Often people believe that, since financial security is good, financial risk must be bad. But this is false. If you never take a financial risk, it is extremely unlikely that you will ever be financially independent. Risk is the price of opportunity. Often people believe that failure is bad. Wrong. Only a poor man regrets his failures. A rich man learns from his failures.[51]

Guard your credit rating. After all, remember that you are holding a job in order to live and to secure that rating. Keep only one or two credit cards with you and force yourself to use them only for emergencies. (If you drive, however, you may want to keep several gasoline company credit cards as well as an automobile club card with you for emergencies.) Find out your credit rating by contacting your local credit bureau. It will give you the information for a small fee. When you get your rating, see if there are any 'slow pays' or other abnormalities on it; if there are, contact the company involved and see if you can get them removed. Avoid developing the insidious habit of relying on your plastic money for your purchases. If you doubt the importance of this advice, ask any banker. He'll probably be able to tell you any number of sad stories.

2. *Create an investment fund.* The justification for this is that the best way to become financially independent is to use money to make money. The purpose of your investment fund is to provide money for your initial investments. It need not be a lot of money, but it should be at least five thousand dollars. Double that would be better. But where are you to get that much money?

In the usual ways. You may be able to create your investment fund by selling some of your unnecessary assets, for example, an expensive automobile or boat. You may be able to create it by saving more money from each paycheck. You may be able to create it by taking a part-time job on weekends or evenings. You may be able to create it by finding a way to profit from your hobby.

There is at least one method for creating it that requires no seed money at all. This method relies on other people's need

157

to unwind. A talented person can cater to that need by, for example, writing a best selling book. According to Ralph Daigh, founding publisher of Fawcett World Library, Crest, Gold Medal, and Premier Books, "there is, and always has been, an absolute dearth of, lack of, paucity of superior authors and superior manuscripts".[52] He offers as evidence the hundreds of thousands of *bad* books that are published and sold every year. Publishers yearn for manuscripts that will sell. Just think of all the best selling books that are bad! Do you enjoy reading? Have you sometimes thought, after reading a bestseller, 'I could do better than that'? Are you willing to do your very best to create a readable manuscript? Do you have a recurring desire to write? Are you fascinated by words—their spelling, their shades of meaning, their grammatical combinations? If the answer to these five questions is 'yes', why not give serious consideration to becoming a writer?

If you know what to do with the royalties, just one or two bestsellers will be enough to establish financial independence. Writing a good book is also emotionally satisfying and adds to your social stature.

Writing requires almost no special equipment or training. Applying the seat of your pants to the seat of the chair in front of a writing table for an hour or so everyday is all the time you need. You can think about your book while you are exercising or commuting back and forth to work or, if your job permits it, even during work. I have held a couple of jobs (twice as a security guard and once as a night clerk/auditor at a motel) that permitted me to write (or to read) while getting paid for it!

Your book can be either fiction or nonfiction. A nonfiction

book in almost any field is a possibility if your background has made you an expert. If you are able to translate your expertise into readily understandable, everyday language, you have a good chance for success. Consider Robert Townsend's *Up The Organization*. Townsend was a successful businessman who had never before written a book. Yet Fawcett paid him a guaranteed advance against royalties of $275,000 (in 1970 dollars) for paperback reprint rights! Besides the good advice that it contains, its chief virtue is its nontechnical, readily intelligible language. Had he chosen to communicate the same ideas in a dense, heavily footnoted, bureaucratic prose, and had it attracted a publisher at all, it would only have been enjoyed by a handful of business school teachers. Even if such a book were competitively priced, nobody would have felt a need to buy it, despite its worthy message. You must keep your audience in mind as you write and, if you want to sell a large number of books, you must use ordinary, nontechnical language.

If your book is a novel, it need not be a beautifully written literary masterpiece. It need only be clearly written, quickly paced, and a good story. To learn what sells, simply read the last ten books that have been number one bestsellers. They are readily available as inexpensive paperbacks if they are not in your local library. Study their similarities. Keep a written record for your own use. When you write your novel, write it in your own way, but it probably won't hurt if you have features in it that are similar to the ones on your list.

I doubt that the craft of writing can be taught. Once, when Somerset Maugham addressed a friend's English literature class, a student asked him how to write a novel. He replied,

"There are three rules for the writing of a novel. Unfortunately no one knows what they are.".[53]

Helpful aids nevertheless exist for writers. In addition to a good dictionary (I recommend *The Compact Edition of the Oxford English Dictionary*), a guide to English grammar, the latest edition of *Roget's International Thesaurus*, and the latest edition of *Fowler's Modern English Usage*, I recommend the latest edition of *The Writers's Handbook*, which should be available in your local library. It contains, among other useful features, helpful tips on writing fiction. I also suggest with respect to fiction Robert C. Meredith's and John D. Fitzgerald's *Structuring Your Novel: From Basic Idea to Finished Manuscript* to help you get past sticking points.

The most important aid for any writer is a healthy ego. A writer must care passionately about his work. It is difficult to care very much about something without working hard on it. (Think of a love affair.) You are unlikely to work hard on any project without believing that the final result will be worth the effort. A writer with a healthy ego will believe that his final product will be worthy of his best efforts. A writer with a healthy ego will also be better able than a writer with a weak ego to handle the rejections from publishers and agents (and there are likely to be many). If you know that your book is a good one, then you will also know that anyone who rejects it will be making a mistake.

The only way for a writer to develop a justifiably healthy ego is to work hard at the craft of writing. This means caring about every sentence, about every word. If you would be a writer, ask yourself George Orwell's questions: What am I trying to say? What words will express it? What image or idiom will make it clearer? Is this image fresh enough to have an effect? Could I put it more shortly? Have I said anything avoidably ugly?

Depending upon the professor, a course or two in creative writing may be helpful. A good writing teacher will be a good editor, a good critic. You can teach yourself how to rewrite what you have written—and everyone knows that rewriting is the secret of writing well. You'll be fortunate indeed to find a good editor—whether a writing teacher or an author or a professional editor. Friends, spouses, and relatives are unlikely to be good editors, but they may be good copy editors. An author usually has little choice but to rely on his own best judgment.

What works for me is to write the first draft quickly and uncritically. Then I rewrite, let it 'cool', and revise again and again. Think hard about each sentence—at least after you have written it! Thinking about it too hard in advance can cause stagnation ('writer's block'). Careful thinking is the hard part of good writing. Careful thinking doesn't just happen: it takes ability and hard work. As Leon Uris wrote somewhere, "In short, one must apply the seat of one's pants to the seat of the chair and write. There is no other way." It is difficult. But as Spinoza tells us in the last sentence of his *Ethics*, "all noble things are as difficult as they are rare".[54]

If this idea of writing for profit intrigues you, I suggest that, minimally, you do a bit more reading about it. The most intellectually respectable work is Coser, Kadushin, and Powell's *Books: The Culture and Commerce of Publishing*. (All authors should at least read chapters 5, 9, and 11.) The best book of practical advice is probably still Appelbaum and Evans's *How to Get Happily Published*.

Just as in making a friend or having a love affair or winning a lottery, there is an element of luck in writing a financially profitable book: success is beyond your own control. Perhaps, as Aristotle argues,[55] this is a sufficient reason for not attempting to make it the meaning of your life, but it is not, by itself, a sufficient reason for not trying it at all. If we always avoided engaging in an activity where success was beyond our own control, we would never try, for example, to create a friendship or a love affair. How could a person lead a blessed life without love? Living well can be a risky business. Isn't it more interesting that way?

It is not true that it takes money to make money. It is possible, for example, for a talented, hard working, and initially impoverished writer to write his way to financial independence. On the other hand, financial independence is easier if one starts with some money. (The money that you start with need not even be your own.)

3. *Develop a plan for investing your investment fund.* Suppose that your reserve fund is full and that your investment fund has five or ten thousand dollars in it. Is there some best way to turn this money into a sufficiently large endowment?

There are all sorts of ways to invest that money. You could invest in precious metals or gems, or purchase art or other collectibles. You could let it earn interest in a savings account at the bank. You could invest in treasury bills, money market funds, common stocks, bonds, commodities, mutual funds, discounted mortgages, commercial real estate (office buildings), residential estate (houses or apartment buildings), rural real estate (farm land), or speculative real estate ('undeveloped' land that you hope will one day be 'developed'). New investment instruments are continually being designed. You could, like Franklin, start your own business. What is the best way to invest your investment fund?

No one way is the best for everyone. I do not propose to try to state the advantages and disadvantages of all the ways possible to invest your money. Instead, I propose to state five general principles for developing your plan and to suggest one sample plan that satisfies them all. The five principles are: [56]

1. Spend your investment money only on goods that are likely to increase in value.
2. Spend your investment money on the best single asset.
3. Be willing to risk your investment money.
4. Maintain control of your investment money.
5. Think in terms of 'real' dollars.

1. *Spend your investment money only on goods that are likely to increase in value.* There are three sorts of goods: those that increase in value over time, those that decrease in value over time, and those that remain the same in value over time. If the value in question is monetary value, which is something like the exchange value of a commodity on the market place, there are few goods that remain the same in value over time—so we may ignore them here. You can, then, spend your investment money on goods that will increase in value over time (for example, some stocks and some real estate) or on goods that will decrease in value over time (for example, an automobile or a boat). Obviously, if you spend your investment money on consumer goods you will dry up

163

your investment fund quickly. Take a vacation in the South Pacific for a month—but give up the idea of financial independence.

If you want financial independence, you must make it your goal. Figure out how much 'real' (in other words, after tax and after inflation and other expenses) money you would need to live as comfortably as you want to live. Would you require $20,000 or $100,000 yearly? Figure it out. Next, determine, at current interest rates, how large your personal endowment must be in order to yield an amount sufficient to support the style of living that you require. Then factor in some reasonable long-term inflation rate. One million dollars or five million dollars? Whatever it is, write it down. That is your goal.

From now on, when you spend money, ask yourself, 'Will this purchase contribute to my goal?' If not, don't buy; if so, buy. If you need something to live (for example, a car to get to work), buy one. But find out how to spend as little money as possible on such purchases. For example, look up in the frequency-of-repair records in *Consumer Reports* magazine on how various kinds of cars hold up and consider buying a good used car. Or, better, buy a sensible new car and maintain it well enough that it will last for 150,000 or 200,000 miles. Don't buy a fancy sports or luxury car simply because you happen to want one. Buy only what you need—not what you want (even if you are able to afford what you want).

2. *Spend your investment money on the best single asset.* There are plenty of assets that are likely to increase in value, for example, stocks and real estate and bonds. You may be tempted to spread your money around among them, to hedge your bets, to diversify. Don't. As Andrew Carnegie is supposed to have said, "Put all your eggs in one basket—and watch that basket."

The reason is that you don't have very much money. Suppose that you have $5,000. If you spread it around, you will wind up with only a small amount of money in everything. For example, suppose that you put your money into a mutual fund and that the manager of that fund spends your money to buy about $500 worth of each of ten stocks. Over time, some may greatly increase in value and some may not. Suppose that one stock really does take off. You only have $500 invested in it. How much money are you really going to make with such a small initial investment?

The time to diversify is after you have accumulated wealth—not when you are just starting out. In the beginning, concentrate your wealth on the best *single* investment. This will give you the maximum opportunity to increase your wealth.

3. *Be willing to risk your investment money.* It is, of course, safer to spread your money around, but there is no perfectly safe way to become wealthy. Do not be inordinately concerned about your financial security. For now, let your job and your reserve fund provide your security. (If you are well-prepared to work and a good employee, even if you lose your job you will be able to get another one.) Your investment money is for your long-term, not short-term, security. If you are unwilling to risk it, it is unlikely that you will ever become wealthy. To continue the example from the previous paragraph, suppose that you had had all your investment money riding on that one stock that did take off. This would have been much riskier than spreading your money around, but the payoff with $5,000 invested would have been much greater than with only $500 invested. Without risk there is unlikely to be any terrific rate of return.

This is not to say that you should risk it foolishly. Spend it only on a calculated risk. This brings me to the most important principle.

4. *Maintain control of your investment money.* You have worked hard for your investment money. Do you really think that it is wise to give it to someone else to spend? There are plenty of people who would like to spend your money for you. They would love for you to turn over your money to them. And they'll even take a profit for spending it for you!

Your own judgment is as good as anyone else's. If it isn't, develop it. Start by taking out of the library some of the many good money management books. Or enroll in a basic money management course at your local college. The bother of doing this is less than the alternative of turning over your money to someone else. It is very unlikely that you'll become wealthy by turning over all your money to some investment counselor. (If that investment counselor was so good at making money, why is he still working at a job like that?)

Neither you, nor anyone else, will ever fully understand the U.S. economy (much less the world economy). It is simply too complex, which is one reason why it is so fascinating. No one has ever known, for example, what was going to happen next in the stock market, so don't buy stocks. There are too many unknown variables. Buying stock is simply giving your money to someone else by buying a piece of a company that someone else runs. Put your eggs in your own basket. You can find investments more stable than the stock market.

Even if you wanted to give your investment fund to an expert to invest, how would you select such an expert?

166

Suppose, for example, that you have a wealthy uncle who successfully runs his own business and that you are tempted to invest in his company because you know that in the past he has been an excellent businessman. Will the future continue to resemble the past? Will he continue to make excellent decisions in running his business? One never knows. There may be adverse market forces beyond his control. If you give him the money, you'll be on the sidelines sweating out the outcome of the game. Wouldn't you really rather be a player than a spectator?

I would. I'd rather let my own decisions determine what happens to my investment money. Perhaps this is just a character flaw! But I simply don't want to turn my investment money over to just anybody and I don't know how to pick an expert. My only alternative is to maintain control myself.

5. *Think in terms of 'real' dollars.* Invest in something that will be likely to grow at a wealth-producing rate. Mere growth is not enough. An investment that does not grow fast enough will be eaten up by inflation and taxes. Think in terms of 'real' dollars—because those are the only kind that can be spent.

What, then, might constitute an adequate, sample plan? Again, the key to becoming wealthy is to provide a product or service that satisfies a felt need at a competitive price. There is no one correct answer. You may have some extraordinary ability that can be used to create financial independence; if so, use it. You may happen to have a large investment fund instead of a small one; if so, you may be in a position to select less risky initial investments. You may be able to take over a small family business with the knowledge that you can quickly expand it, increase its profits and then sell it; if so, why not do that?

But suppose that you are a person with average ability, a small investment fund, and without special circumstances. What should you do? My suggestion is to consider investing in residential real estate.

All people feel a need for a place to live. If you provide them with housing to rent from you, you will be satisfying a felt need. If you buy your property wisely, you will be able to provide an apartment or house for someone to rent at or below competitive market price. Providing a good place to live at or below the competitive price enables you to attract good tenants. If you treat your tenants well and attract good tenants to begin with, you will have few headaches as a property manager (landlord). The rents that your tenants pay will build your equity in the property. This equity will eventually make you financially independent.

Notice that the demand for a place to live does not fluctuate with the economic times; everyone must live somewhere whether or not the general economy is growing. That fact creates demand in real estate. Forget about commercial, rural, or speculative real estate. Forget about every investment but one: housing people. It is only by specializing that you will be able to control your own financial destiny and become wealthy. It is true that nobody understands the whole economy, but parts of it can be understood. Consider making it your initial task to understand your local market in residential real estate.

What kind of housing do people need? They do not need luxury apartments or oceanside condominiums or expensive mansions—even though these, too, are residential real estate.

People may want luxury housing, but they ought not to feel a need for it (and usually don't) because they cannot afford it. People feel a need for affordable, three-bedroom, two-bathroom houses in good condition in stable neighborhoods. Think in terms of quiet, working class neighborhoods. What kind of a neighborhood would you want to live in? It would be quiet—so forget about houses on busy streets or near commercial corners. Yet it would be a neighborhood that is near good public transportation, good schools, good shopping districts, and good parks. It would be clean, safe, and well-maintained. It would not be a neighborhood of the least expensive houses; it would be a neighborhood of medium-priced houses, houses in the $45,000 to $75,000 price range. Think of demand as like a cone: there's lots of demand (size) at the bottom and very little demand (size) at the top.

So the first step is to determine where, within ten miles, there is such a neighborhood near you. (If there isn't one, you'll have to do something else in residential real estate. This is actually my situation; I live in a recreational/rural area that is devoid of working-class neighborhoods or suburbs. But I still have been able to own and manage two apartment buildings in addition to my own house.) Then learn the market. Subscribe to your local paper and spend 20 minutes or so every day going over the real estate listings. Spend a couple of hours every Sunday stopping in open houses in your chosen neighborhood. You are learning about the market in your chosen specialty. There is no substitute for knowing that market. Ask any businessman.

You will notice that the real estate market is not perfectly competitive in terms of price or financing. You are less concerned with price than with financing: you must arrange it in the beginning so that your expenses (mortgage payment, insurance, taxes, repairs, utilities [if any], and so on) are less than your income from rents; if they are, you will have a positive cash flow. If they are not, you will have a negative cash flow or you will break even. You want at least to break even.

Even if you only break even from month-to-month, you will really be gaining in other ways. First, as each month passes, you will own a little more of your property, in other words, your equity will be growing. Other people's money (their rents) will be paying off your mortgage. Second, you'll be benefitting on your taxes. Think of it this way: the government knows that people need housing. It has two choices: it can provide such housing itself or it can arrange the tax code in such a way that private investors will be encouraged to provide housing. The problem with the former method is that governments are not organized like businesses and, so, they tend to do a poor job of either building or managing housing. It is much better for the government to arrange the tax code so that private investors will be encouraged to build and to manage housing. Of course, you are not a builder; you will simply buy previously existing housing and manage it. The tax breaks are not now as good as they were several years ago, but they are not nonexistent. For example, *if* you have selected a good property to purchase, it will go up in value each year. Its value should increase as much as the inflation rate; it will be worth more when you sell it than it was when you purchased it. But the federal tax code pretends that the building is decreasing in value; it lets the real estate investor depreciate the building each year, in other words, pretend for tax purposes that the building is wearing out. The

170

government pretends that the building is decreasing in value when it is in reality increasing in value! It does this not because it is stupid, but because it wants to encourage private investors to provide housing. This can help to create your fortune. There are other tax breaks as well. Many of the property-related expenses are tax deductible. You may, for example, buy a real estate book, hire an accountant to do your taxes, pay a telephone bill for your business phone, or hire a plumber to fix a sink in a building that you own. All these are dollar-for-dollar deductions, in other words, your taxable income is reduced by one dollar for each dollar that you spend. Your accountant can help you to find other legal vehicles such as IRAs and incorporating that will help you to reduce your taxes. Why pay more in taxes than is necessary?

If you have any special skills, you may be able to tailor your purchases to them. If, for example, you are a painter, plumber, or electrician, or if you know how to install dry wall, carpeting, or roofing, you can specialize in buying otherwise sound houses that match your skills. You may find a sound house in an excellent location that simply needs exterior painting and, because of that obvious need, is underpriced. If you have the time, energy, and ability to do the painting yourself, that may be just the house for you to buy.

There are different ways to proceed even in medium-priced residential real estate. The right person could, for example, buy the house that I just described, repaint it, and sell it immediately at a profit. This is the 'fixer-upper' approach. You can specialize in fixing-up houses cosmetically or redoing outdated kitchens or converting built-in garages into extra bedrooms. Do this a few times successfully and you'll really see your investment fund grow.

A mistake in real estate can cost you thousands of dollars. So crack the books before beginning in order to minimize your chances of making a mistake. If we didn't learn from others, we'd still be living in caves. There is no one book that will have all the information that you need. Get information from several books. (I've listed some in the bibliography.) Before purchasing property you should teach yourself about four things: neighborhoods, houses, financing, and sellers.

The most important feature of housing is its location. What, in general, makes a good location? Demand. The demand may not be where you think it is. You might think that there is demand for housing in neighborhoods with very expensive houses. That is not so. Most people cannot afford to live in affluent suburbs. They feel a need to live in a neighborhood like that I previously described. They don't want a neighborhood that shows signs of blight (for example, peeling house paint, missing roof shingles, sagging porches, or overgrown lawns). Train yourself to observe such features. Is the house that you are looking to buy the least expensive house in the neighborhood? If so, it may be the best deal. Avoid the most expensive house in the neighborhood; its value will increase less relative to the other houses. And force yourself to learn about important factors that are not readily observable, for example, future population changes and economic forecasts.

Educate yourself about what physical aspects to look for. The best book about repair and maintenance of houses is *Petersen's Home Repair and Maintenance Guide.* It contains a thorough inspection guide in its opening chapter. You need to know how to examine the house's exterior, basement, windows, walls, ceilings, floors, plumbing, heating system, and electrical system. If the property is in less than excellent condition, you must be able to determine the approximate cost to put it in excellent condition.

There is no substitute here for experience. In fact, one way to learn is to buy an older house in poor condition and fix it up. Do that once and you'll forever be good at spotting work that needs to be done and estimating the time and materials that it will cost to restore a house to excellent condition. Consider this knowledge part of your expertise as a real estate investor. It may cost you a few thousand dollars to gain it, but no worthy education is inexpensive. Minimize your cost by learning as much as you can from others, for example, by reading the relevant literature. (The books in the Time/Life *Home Repair and Improvement* series are also useful.)

Find a banker willing to talk with you about financing, preferably one who invests in residential real estate. Tell him that you are ignorant about real estate investing but that you are eager to learn. And listen. Then go to your public library and read some more.

Look for a seller who is desperate to unload the sort of house that you are looking for. You are looking for a seller who will be flexible about the financial terms. In return for good terms, you'll be able to afford to give him the fair market price for his home. So you both win. In other words, you are looking for a highly motivated seller. Find a seller who has just retired and desperately wants to sell his house immediately and move to Florida. Or a seller who just needs to sell because he has money problems or tax problems. Or someone who wants to sell immediately because his company has just transferred him to a job in another state. Or a seller who is a real estate investor wanting to unload a property because its

173

depreciation has run out. Such people can be found, although they may be only about one or two percent of the sellers on the market at any one time. There are ways to find them. Real estate books can advise you about locating such people. The best sellers are the kind who will hold a mortgage themselves. This avoids banks completely—and avoids paying for the profits that a bank will take. This is why it is important to establish a good credit rating. Whether a private seller or a bank finances you, you'll need to have a good credit rating to begin to buy residential real estate.

Have you ever heard of anyone losing money in moderately priced residential real estate? It has happened, but it is infrequent, even for inexperienced persons. Spend three to six months researching; don't, for example, rush out and buy after reading only one or two books. But begin constructing a concrete plan.

Get a lawyer who knows about real estate transactions, preferably one who is himself a real estate investor. As Bruce Williams always emphasizes, never sign a purchase offer without first having consulted your own attorney. In your initial meeting, ask him to give you a blank purchase offer form so that you can study it. From the real estate literature that you have been reading you'll know what sorts of clauses to add to it to protect yourself. For example, you will want to write a purchase offer so that the purchase price you are paying is not more than the appraisal price given by a professional appraiser.

You may consider finding a house by going through a real estate broker, but remember that, unless you make unusual arrangements in advance, the broker works for the seller—not for you, the buyer.

174

Plan to put down not less than five percent and not more than ten percent of the property's price. Your attorney can help you to figure out the closing costs in advance. These will be much lower if you avoid bank financing. Remember to increase your reserve fund by the appropriate amount.

4. *Execute your plan.* Your first piece of residential real estate will be your most difficult to acquire. I recommend that you begin by buying yourself a house to live in that will eventually make a good rental property. There is nothing to be gained by buying the most expensive house you can afford. Simply buy a decent house in a good location and, if necessary, fix it up until it is in excellent condition. Once that house is ready, look for another; buy it, rent out the first, and repeat the process. With practice, you'll get better and better at finding motivated sellers, assessing buildings, writing purchase offers, fixing up buildings, and managing tenants.

You should revise your plan according to your own experience and with an eye on your own changing circumstances. Once you have purchased your first house, your practical experience can supplement the experience you gained from reading books. It isn't very intellectually difficult to tailor your plan to your own circumstances. For example, if you are not handy with tools, or prefer not to bother with them, you should buy only buildings that are in excellent condition. Decide whether or not you are going to manage tenants yourself or hire someone else to do it. If you plan to pay someone else to do it, you'll have to figure in that additional cost in the beginning. If you do it yourself, you'll have to develop several forms to use: an application to rent form, a property condition inspection form, a lease/rental agreement form, and so on. Your own forms can easily be

175

made from the real estate books; it is a good idea to give them to your attorney for his suggestions before you use them.

There are two potential major problems about being a real estate investor. One is that your money is tied up in real estate; it is not 'liquid'. You cannot spend equity. The best way to minimize this difficulty is to buy only properties for which there is a demand. Such properties sell quickly. Furthermore, the real estate books can teach you how to sell real estate properly yourself, which will increase the chances for a quick sale.

The other is handling tenants. It is actually fun trying to buy good properties, trying to construct deals that are in the best interests of both oneself and the seller. And fixing up a property is satisfying work. But it is sometimes no fun dealing with tenants. There is a real art to it. You will need to attract good tenants, have them complete applications to rent, check out the information that they provide, collect sizeable deposits in advance, have them sign complete, legally binding leases or rental agreements, and ensure that all provisions of those contracts are kept.

The way to minimize the difficulty is i. to be prepared in advance and ii. to give good value. *i.* I have observed that many people who try it are simply unprepared to be good landlords. They don't know the first thing about it and they make it much more difficult than it has to be. The way to be prepared is to teach yourself how to be a landlord. It sounds like an obvious first step, but people are often foolish. I recommend two books. The best is: Leigh Robinson's *Landlording*; it is extremely useful. Another good one is Albert J. Lowry's *How to Manage Real Estate Successfully—in your Spare Time*. Read one or, better, both from cover to cover

176

before you begin. *ii.* The real secret is to have good tenants—ones who pay their rents promptly and without fail, who keep the property in excellent condition, who don't disturb their neighbors, and who are willing to do a bit of troubleshooting on occasion for themselves. The only way to attract and to keep such tenants is to give good value. The house or apartment must be in excellent condition. You must keep your agreements, including prompt attention to any required or promised improvements. Your rental unit should also be in a desirable location and priced at, or (better) below, market rent.

I have suggested that at least once you ought to fix up an older house in order to teach yourself how to be a better real estate investor. Similarly, it is also a good idea to manage a property at least once for a year or so in order to teach yourself how to be a better real estate investor. If you are able to do it yourself, you will be in a position to judge how others do it later. So if you eventually hire a plumber to replace a toilet or hire a real estate management company to manage your properties, you'll be able to satisfy yourself that you are getting good value for your dollar.

Complete your own long-term plan. You may, for example, want to purchase one house each year for 15 years. At the end of the time, you can sell all your houses, diversify your assets, and live happily ever after. Figure out exactly what you are doing before you get started, but don't be so inflexible that change becomes impossible. You may wish, for example, to buy an apartment house if you happen upon an excellent deal rather than buying the single-family, detached house that you had planned to buy. Buy and continue to buy housing in accordance with that plan. Knowledge is useless unless used.

You may generate a terrific plan for becoming financially independent but, if you fail to act, you will fail to become financially independent. People who become so paralyzed by fear of making a mistake that they do not act are people who are paralyzed. The goal is financial independence, not paralysis.

Learn from your mistakes. You will probably make many mistakes about your investments. Anticipate them. Keep your reserve fund for emergencies. And grin and bear it. Just resolve never to make the same mistake twice.

There is a way to learn how to manage residential real estate without owning it. Suppose that you would like to learn how to be a property manager and do not yet have enough money to buy anything for yourself. Here's an idea: look for a position as a property manager. It can be a full- or part-time position. You'll learn about managing a building and tenants.

For example, suppose that you have a job and now live in an apartment that costs you, say, $400 monthly in rent. Think about the following. Find a part-time job as a property manager in a small apartment building. Suppose that you find a position in a building with six apartments and you arrange to live in the building at a discounted rent. Suppose that an apartment rents in that building for $400 but you will get it for $100 monthly plus your duties as building manager. You can sock an extra $300 monthly into your investment fund while you are learning the business! Furthermore, you will come in contact with a real estate investor, the person who owns the building, and learn what he does. You might even wind up owning that apartment building when the investor decides to sell. If he likes you, you may get some really good terms. Why not take a part-time job that will go a long way towards furthering your goal of financial independence?

This goal, however, is not itself the overall goal. Financial independence is not the meaning of life. What is?

9
The Meaning of Life

There are some who claim that life has no meaning. Life is terminal; death is inevitable. How, then, could it possibly have any meaning? All our Projects, however nobly intended, conceived and executed, will ultimately be overwhelmed. Everything is futile. All is pointless.

Even the evidence of modern cosmological speculation seems to point toward this position. When Newton published his great *Principia* in 1687 he expounded his concept of Universal Gravitation. But he left one obvious question unanswered. Since all the stars and planets are attracting each other, why don't they collapse together into one grand fiery ball? It took about two centuries for anyone to make a significant step toward answering this question. In 1888 H. C. Vogel discovered the Doppler effect in starlight. The Doppler effect is a change in wavelength that is observable when the source of the wavelength (radiation), for example, sound or light, is moving. If the source is moving toward the observer, the wavelength is shortened; if it is moving away, the wavelength is lengthened. Vogel discovered that the whole spectrum of starlight is shifted towards the longer, or red, end of the white light spectrum.

Many galaxies are like pinwheels of stars. In the 1920s Vesto Slipher discovered that the light from virtually all galaxies displays a 'red-shift'. Edwin Hubble determined that the degree of 'red-shift' is directly proportional to the distances of the galaxies: the farther away from us a galaxy is, the greater the 'red-shift.' With the exception of a dozen or so galaxies in our own cosmic neighborhood, every galaxy seems to be rushing away from every other galaxy. They are rushing apart at velocities that are proportional to their distances: the farther away a galaxy is from us, the faster it is moving away from us. In other words, the universe is expanding.

This is where the myth of the 'Big Bang' comes from. If today the galaxies are all rushing apart from each other, then yesterday they must have been closer together. And the day before yesterday they must have been even closer together. And so on. So it seems reasonable to assume that once upon a time there was a grand explosion that created our expanding universe. (The physicist George Gamow rather irreverently called it the 'big bang'.) If a grenade is exploded in the air, its fragments will fly apart in all directions. The Big Bang was like such a grenade explosion; the galaxies are like its fragments.

If this Big Bang myth is correct, what may we hope for? There are only three alternatives. First, the universe will keep expanding until the expansion simply runs down. A state of entropy will be reached in which all chemical reactions will cease. Since life depends upon chemical reactions, this would mean the permanent extinction of all life. No human or nonhuman forms of life would remain. Even if a human product (for example, a statue) were to survive, there would be no one to appreciate it.

Second, the force of gravity will eventually overcome the force of the Big Bang. Think of a rubber ball on an elastic string hit by a wooden paddle: the ball is like a galaxy and the elastic is like gravity. Hit the ball and it will stretch the elastic— but only to a certain point. Then the elastic will pull the ball back towards the paddle. If this happens to the universe, it will eventually stop expanding and start collapsing. It will all fall together into one grand 'black hole'. This, too, would mean the extinction of all life in the universe.

Third, the expansion is permanent. This so-called 'steady-state' theory depends upon the spontaneous generation of matter from nothing. Matter is constantly being created and forced out from a cosmic epicenter. The universe is expanding now. It always will expand. This view entails the permanent possibility of life. But there are three problems with it. First, how can matter constantly be generated from nothing? Second, if matter were somehow constantly generated from nothing, galaxies would be of different ages. But all the nearby galaxies, at least, seem to be the same age. Because of the difficulties in overcoming these two objections, most cosmologists today reject the 'steady-state' theory. Third, even though life may exist permanently, it may not. The possibility that it may not cease to exist does not exclude the possibility that it may cease to exist.

If the cosmologists are correct, we may reasonably predict either entropy or a cosmic black hole. It makes no difference. Even if, for example, one of my works were to survive my death, it would make no difference in the long run if these are the only two alternatives. Nothing ever done by any human, even an Alexander the Great, will have any permanent significance. It begins to seem, then, as if everything really is futile.

For what I am about in this chapter, it does not matter whether or not any of the cosmological theories just mentioned, or anything even like them, are adequate. (As with all scientific theories, there are anomalies and unanswered questions. For example, why is the universe lumpy?) What matters is the problem of the meaning of human life that they may be used to suggest. Do our lives have any meaning? Can our lives have any meaning?

Assume the worst; hope for the best. That is usually a wise rule of thumb. For the sake of the argument, let us assume the worst. In the present context, this means making two assumptions.

First, assume that each of us will soon die. Being dead is the opposite of being alive. Being alive is something; being dead is nothing. Each of us is mortal. Even if, for example, my life has meaning for me, there will soon be no such meaning because I shall soon not exist.

Second, assume that everything human will someday cease to exist. If so, each of us is mortal in a second sense: nothing we ever do or think will permanently exist. It is not just that each of us will cease to exist; it is that all traces of us will cease to exist. Whether beneficial or detrimental, all the effects of our Projects will cease to exist.

Reflections like these stimulate people like Tolstoy to thoughts of suicide. He wrote: "I want to know the meaning of life, but the fact that it is a particle of the infinite not only gives it no meaning, but even destroys every possible meaning".[57] To reasonable questions concerning the meaning of life, Tolstoy himself decided to become unreasonable. He tried to give up rationality in favor of irrationality. He tried to retreat to the domain of blind faith in the supernatural. However popular this endeavor, I cannot sanction it. Reasonable questions demand either reasonable answers or the honest admission of ignorance. Fantastical answers are irrelevant.

What if our lives have no cosmic significance? What if our lives are pointless? What if the only point of living is simply to be living? What if our lives have no external source of meaning?

There are two significant reactions to this idea. The first is bitter disapppointment. After all, just living is a full-time Project that, for most people, lasts for decades; it involves intense concern if not dedicated effort. Many of us would like a cosmic father to pat us on the head and tell us that we are doing just fine, that we are successfully completing his great plan for us. We may not know why we are doing what we are doing, but he must! True, many other animals who share our planet also seem to toil ceaselessly, generation after generation. But aren't we special? Yes, in many ways we are special (see the next chapter). But we are not special in the required sense. Neither the life of an ant nor the life of a human has any cosmic significance. There is no cosmic significance.

It is impossible to prove such a negative proposition. But thinking that it needs proof is backwards: the burden of proof falls upon anyone who holds that life has a cosmic significance. If this affirmative claim is not justified by evidence, it is worthless. Where is the evidence? I know of none. Someone, tomorrow, may present some; however unlikely, it may happen. Until tomorrow comes, the choice is to be rational or irrational. I prefer rationality; I prefer to leave conceptual illusions to others. They will retort that I am intellectually blind. Decide for yourself. The second significant reaction is one of relief. We are free from cosmic entanglements! Our lives are our own; they belong to nobody else. If we get the blame when our affairs go badly, we also get the praise when they go well. This is why Nietzsche thought that the death of God was liberating rather than deplorable.[58]

Even if it is true that our lives have no cosmic meaning, it does not follow that they have no meaning. Even if God doesn't infuse our lives with meaning, perhaps, at the risk of playing God, we can render our own lives meaningful. A meaningful life need not have cosmic significance. It also need not have permanent significance. All that it needs to have is meaning.

Even if it were true that our lives have no meaning, it does not follow that it is false that life is an abstract good. In Chapter 4 I distinguished concrete from abstract existents, individuals from properties. I suggested that goodness was a property of properties; if so, some properties such as pleasure, life, knowledge, and beauty are abstract goods. Concrete existents exemplify different properties. Insofar as a concrete existent exemplifies an abstract good, it is (indirectly) good; insofar as a concrete existent exemplifies an abstract evil, it is (indirectly) evil. It is at least theoretically possible for a concrete existent to exemplify both an abstract good and an abstract evil simultaneously. This is one of two reasons why it is wise always to be cautious in attributing goodness to a concrete existent; that same individual may simultaneously (in a different way) be evil. An act of murder, for example, takes away the victim's life, which is why it is evil; at the same time, however, the murderer may derive pleasure from the act and pleasure is an abstract good. Of course, since the victim's life is more important than the murderer's pleasure, the act as a whole may be correctly judged to be evil. But the evaluation may not be as simple as it seems at first glance. Real-life evaluations of concrete existents are sometimes very complicated. And such complicated cases may be used to raise the question about knowing how to rank abstract goods.

The second reason why it is always wise to be cautious in attributing goodness to a concrete existent is that mistake in such attributions is always possible. Surely, for example, the consequences of an action are relevant to its evaluation. But isn't it impossible to know *all* the consequences of some actions in advance? Someone could argue with some plausibility that the murder of Hitler prior to the start of World War II would have been, on balance, good, that the evil of the act itself would have been outweighed by its good consequences. The difficulty, of course, is that the potential murderer (assassin!) could not have known in advance that, for example, Hitler would not change his mind about ordering the invasion of Poland. In general, it is possible to know relationships between abstract existents without knowing which concrete existents exemplify those abstract existents. For example, it is possible to know that pleasure is a good without knowing whether, on balance, a certain act that exemplifies pleasure is (indirectly) good. This is a bit like that fact that it is possible to know that red is a color without knowing whether this shirt is red (because of the impossibility of knowing that you are perceiving it correctly).[59] Plato thought that knowledge is about the unchanging and that knowledge about changeable concrete existents is impossible. Isn't it obvious that his position is at least initially plausible?

Life is an abstract good; hence, insofar as some concrete existent exemplifies life, it is (indirectly) good. No concrete existent is *unqualifiedly* good merely because it is living. The good for a whole concrete existent considered solely as a living thing is health, but that particular existent may also exemplify other relevant properties, other abstract goods and evils.

The question of the meaning of life is the question of the purpose of life. 'Purpose' is ambiguous.[60] In one sense, a purpose is what something is *for*, for example, if God created all living creatures for the purpose of glorifying Himself. Does all of life have a purpose in this sense? Are all living beings *for* something? I think not. In this sense of 'purpose', life has no purpose beyond itself. But it does not follow that life is meaningless.

In a second sense, a purpose is a goal. For example, your exercising may have as its goal attaining a higher level of fitness. In this sense of 'purpose', your life will have whatever purpose you choose, namely, your Project(s). A life without a Project would be a life without a purpose (a meaning). Since some goals are better than others and since different lives may exemplify various goals to different degrees, some human lives may be better than others.

In the tradition of the great chain of being,[61] some lives are probably better than others. For example, because this dog is sentient as well as alive and this dandelion lacks sentience, this dog's life is better than this dandelion's life. They are the same with respect to life, but they differ with respect to the abstract good of sentience. To claim that the one concrete existent (this dog's life) is not better than the other concrete existent (this dandelion's life) would be to ignore that important difference between them. On the other hand, both are good insofar as they are alive, insofar as they are (indirectly) good because they exemplify the abstract good of life. Again, it is always possible that such judgments about concrete existents may be mistaken.

Thinkers such as Plato, Aristotle, and Nietzsche claim that such a hierarchy also applies within our own species: the life of a certain human may be better than the life of a certain other human. Even if correct, notice two important points that do not follow. First, it does not follow that we should actually treat some humans better than we treat other humans. The reason for this is, second, that it does not follow that we can recognize which humans (which concrete existents) are more valuable than which others. Since we cannot know this, we lack any justification for treating one human differently from the way we treat another.

I do not think that we have any reliable means for recognizing the true value of others. We would have to know not only which abstract existents are good and which are evil, but we would also have to know *all* the abstract existents exemplified by the whole of someone's life and that is impossible. As my hero T. E. Lawrence once wrote, "It's my experience that the actual work or position or reward one has, doesn't have much effect on the inner being which is the important thing for us to cultivate." It does not follow that someone is great, for example, simply because they have power or wealth or status. How could we reliably judge the 'inner being' of others? Nietzsche himself claimed that "the greatest thoughts are the greatest events".[62] If so, since we lack

189

a reliable means for recognizing what others are thinking, we lack a reliable means of gauging their value.

This entire conception is quite natural and not at all as strange as it initially may appear. If you had to choose between the destruction of a pebble and the destruction of a flower, wouldn't you choose to destroy the pebble? If you had to choose between the destruction of a flower and the destruction of a ladybug, wouldn't you choose to destroy the flower? If you had to choose between the destruction of a ladybug and the destruction of a dog, wouldn't you choose to destroy the ladybug? If you had to choose between the destruction of a dog and the destruction of a human, wouldn't you choose to destroy the dog? If you had to choose between the destruction of a great human being and the destruction of a less-than-great human being (assuming that you could tell the difference), wouldn't you choose to destroy the less-than-great one?

Of course, such a choice would be horrible. The reaction of the faithful Christian to such a choice would probably be like the reaction of Sonya in *Crime and Punishment* when Raskolnikov put a similar question to her: she wouldn't choose.[63] Nobody would want to choose. Again, it is not possible to recognize which humans are more valuable than which other humans. But if you did, somehow, know and you were forced to choose, isn't the rational choice to destroy the less-than-great one?

The problem of the meaning of life should not be approached abstractly: it should be approached concretely. First and foremost, I am concerned with the meaning, if any, of my life. How can I make it more meaningful? A vague answer begins to emerge: by being all that I can be. By being as great as possible. By making my life as valuable as I am able to make it. By making my experiences exemplify as many important abstract goods as possible.

If we include thinking as an activity, we can correctly think of our lives as a sequence of activities. If some human lives are better than other human lives, then some sequences of activities are better than other sequences of activities.

Deliberately intended, long-term activities are what I have been calling 'Projects'. Each of us has many Projects. A person might, for example, be an artist, a lover, a mother, a friend, a volunteer social worker, a reserve Army officer, an athlete, a diner, and a birder. Some lives are filled with more different Projects than other lives. The life of the busy woman just mentioned might be quite different from the life of a lonely, solitary composer. Some Projects are better than other Projects. A life dedicated to healing the sick is better than a life of burglary and robbery as a means to feed a drug addiction.

Permit me to oversimplify in the name of more felicitous expression and talk as if a single life were dominated by a single Project. Suppose that you were, as you are, confronted with the task of making your life as meaningful as possible by choosing the best possible Project. Which Project should you choose?

I have four suggestions.

1. The Project must be defensible.
2. The good sought must be an end.
3. The Project should be challenging yet possible.
4. The Project should be a continual source of lasting satisfaction.

After briefly considering these four criteria in turn, I give two specific examples of kinds of Projects that satisfy them.

1. *The Project must be defensible.* By 'defensible' I mean 'able to withstand rational scrutiny'. An indefensible Project is an indefensible life, a wasted life. When you are on your deathbed and thinking back over your life, would you want to be in the position of being unable to justify your central Project? Of course not. This is my most important suggestion.

What should I do with my life? What should I try to accomplish? What should be my central Project?

The answer is not obvious. Each of us must decide for himself what to do. Each of us should make a rational decision, in other words, one that would be able to answer all objections raised against it. It would be irrational to accept an answer without being able to justify it, without knowing why you should accept it. There is no easy way to judge the adequacy of any answer.

However, some people claim that there is an easy way out: simply find a moral authority (someone who knows what people should do) and do whatever that being tells you to do. The authority might be a teacher or a priest or a god. For example, an Old Testament prophet said:

> God has told you what is good;
> and what is it that the Lord asks of you?
> Only to act justly, to love loyalty,
> to walk wisely before your God.[64]

There are several serious problems about this. First, it is vague. What exactly is acting justly? How are we to know when we

192

are acting justly? A feeling that we are acting justly is insufficient; Hitler and Stalin, for example, may have felt that they were acting justly when they weren't. Second, does God exist? I know of no sound argument that concludes that the Judeo-Christian God exists. Third, even if God exists, is that what God said? How did Micah know what God said? Have we correctly understood Micah? Fourth, even if this is what God said, how do we know that we have correctly understood it? Jews, Catholics, and Protestants all agree that this is a bit of sacred scripture, but their disagreements concerning interpretations of various scriptural passages are notorious. This way out begins to appear less easy.

It is not even a way out. How do I know that X is a moral authority who should be obeyed? Many beings claim to be moral authorities, and their advice often differs. How should I choose among them? If I am not a moral authority, how can I recognize a moral authority? The rational answer is: I cannot. I must myself be a moral authority in order to recognize a moral authority. But if I were a moral authority, then I would not need to ask another moral authority what to do or what to be.

The responsibility for what you do and for what you are is yours alone. Your task is to make yourself a moral authority. There is no other rational way to do it. Furthermore, this way is difficult. But the only way to be able to give a defensible answer concerning the justification of your central Project is to become a moral authority. Becoming a moral authority involves learning which properties are abstract goods and trying to engage in those concrete activities that are most likely to exemplify the most important abstract goods.

2. *The good sought must be an end.* There is often a difference between the goal (end) of an activity and the means used to attain that goal. For example, having a job may be a means to the goal of being financially independent. In the sometimes hectic hurly-burly of daily life it is possible to concentrate so hard on the means that we lose sight of the end. This is one way of losing control, of being unbalanced, of not having it altogether, of being unwise.

In the first sentence of his *Nicomachean Ethics*, Aristotle points out that "Every art and every inquiry, and similarly every action and choice, is thought to aim at some good".[65] A thought may be correct or incorrect, true or false. You want to have a correct (true) answer to the question about which central Project is best. Furthermore, you should never lose sight of the good that is the end of your central Project. If 'good' always meant only 'good for something else', no Project would ever be justifiable. As Aristotle put it, "If, then, there is some end of the things we do, which we desire for its own sake (everything else being desired for the sake of this), and if we do not choose everything for the sake of something else (for at that rate the process would go on to infinity, so that our desire would be empty and vain), clearly this must be the good and the chief good".[66] The end of your Project should be something that is intrinsically valuable, good in itself, and not something that is only valuable as a means to something else. In other words, the good sought must be an end.

Many abstract existents have been suggested as being intrinsically good. Among them are: wisdom, life, pleasure or satisfaction, happiness, tranquillity, truth, knowledge, beauty, virtue, love, friendship, justice, power, freedom, self expression, peace, excitement, and honor.[67] Some things, such as health, are both intrinsically good and good as a means to other things.

The task, then, is to ensure that your central Project has an intrinsically valuable end as its goal. This rules out, for example, making money as the meaning of life because money is not intrinsically valuable. Each of us should choose an end among the various possible ends. This choice itself, of course, should be justified. Aristotle argues, for example, that life itself should not be the goal because it is not distinctively human, it is common to other animals and even to plants.[68] He also argues against honor because it is too superficial and beyond one's control in the sense that it is bestowed upon one by others.[69]

I know of no sound argument that concludes that there is only one abstract existent that is intrinsically good, only one abstract good. It seems obvious that there are many abstract goods. Even if they all could be systematically ranked in some hierarchical order, it does not follow that all persons should aim at the topmost good. This leads to my next suggestion.

3. *The Project should be challenging yet possible.* It is important to pick a Project that can provide a lifelong challenge. By way of contrast, suppose that I were foolish enough to make my central Project that of becoming financially independent. Such a Project is challenging, but it is not challenging enough. Suppose that I work hard and reach my long-awaited goal at age 50. Then what? Or suppose that I were foolish enough to make my central Project that of raising a brood of children. What am I prepared to do after they have grown up and left home?

On the other hand, it would be foolish to pick an impossible Project. Suppose, for example, that I were foolish

195

enough to want the fame that would come from being a member of a Stanley-Cup-winning Montreal Canadiens hockey team. I simply lack the physical ability to make the team. Had I been foolish enough to make that my Project, I might have wasted years trying to do something that was simply beyond my ability. The same thing would happen if I were foolish enough to want the honor that would accrue to me if I were to become a great physicist like Newton, a great writer like Goethe, a great dramatist like Aeschylus, a great mathematician like Gauss, or a great philosopher like Hume. You are only able to do what you are able to do.

The Project selected should be challenging yet possible. A wise selection will be based on self-knowledge. It would be foolish to select either one that does not provide a lasting challenge or one that provides an impossible challenge. The goal should be set high, perhaps even just beyond your reach, but not too high, not too far beyond your reach. A goal that is too high will be a continual source of frustration and this will eventually dull effort.

Richard Taylor has argued[70] that the best way to think about the meaning of life is to think of it as the opposite of a meaningless life. What would be the best example of a meaningless human life? Recall the myth of Sisyphus. He was condemned by the gods to roll a boulder to the top of a hill. Once at the top, the boulder would roll back down and Sisyphus would have to push it once again to the top. This pointless labor was to continue throughout eternity. Isn't such a life of pointless repetitive effort the best example of a meaningless human life?

In one sense, it may not be. Notice, as Camus points out, that it is open to Sisyphus to adopt an attitude of revolt.[71]

Sisyphus need not try to reconcile himself to his fate: he is free to reject his fate, to adopt an attitude of rebellion, to stand majestically and defiantly in revolt, to understand his condition and to transcend it by scorning it. Sisyphus cannot *do* anything else, but his intellect can raise him above his apparent station. Viewed from without, his life is meaningless; viewed from within, it need not be meaningless.

And there can be one significant difference between our lives and Sisyphus's life: his life must be devoid of creativity while our lives need not be. His circumstances cannot be changed because they have been decreed by the gods. But imagine that they could be changed. Could they be changed in such a way as to make it obvious that his life is meaningful even when viewed from without? Instead of rolling the same boulder up the hill endlessly, let us imagine him rolling different boulders. And let us imagine him using those boulders to create a beautiful temple of his own design. The temple would be a monument to his creativity, a testament to a life well lived, an achievement of a meaningful existence, a concrete existent that exemplified an abstract good. This is why it is so frequently thought that the greatest humans are the greatest creators. This is why it is so easy to admire a Shakespeare, a Beethoven, a Michelangelo, a Plato or an Aeschylus. Their creativity is obvious. It is less obvious, but nevertheless present, in all fields.

My suggestion, then, is that the best kind of Project will involve as much creativity as possible. It is no good trying to be like everyone else, trying to avoid originality as if it were a disease. Try to be your unique self; try to nurture whatever creative power you may have. Find a creative solution to just one of, or one part of, our many serious problems such as the risk of nuclear war, overpopulation, pollution, social injustice or misuse of natural resources and see how your own estimate of your own selfworth soars. This brings me to my final suggestion.

4. *The Project should be a continual source of lasting satisfaction.* Pain should occasion the question, 'What have I been doing wrong?' For example, a headache may mean that I have been under too much stress or that I haven't been eating properly. Pain can lead to changes that can improve life.

Pleasure or satisfaction is surely an ingredient of the best lives. Is it itself a satisfactory goal? One of the problems with making it a goal is that pleasures vary in intensity and duration. Should one seek short, intense pleasures (for example, sexual pleasure) or should one seek longer, less intense pleasures (for example, the pleasure of enjoying a great novel)? Another problem with making it a goal is the so-called hedonistic paradox: if you directly aim at obtaining pleasure, you tend not to obtain it, but if you aim at doing what is good, you tend to obtain pleasure.

Anyone who is engaged in an excellent Project will tend to obtain pleasure or satisfaction from it. Since the Project in question is the central one, it should be longlasting. If an activity is a continual source of lasting satisfaction, that pleasure is a sign that the activity is a good one. The duration of the satisfaction is important; as Aristotle remarks, "one swallow does not make a summer, nor does one day; and so too one day, or a short time, does not make a man blessed and happy"[72]. One desires excellence, which is why it is pleasing when our desires are satisfied; it is not, as Bishop Butler pointed out, that one desires the pleasure and engages in the excellent activity solely as a means to that end.

198

It is important to notice that the goal of a human life may always be questioned. If the end is questionable, the means to it are always questionable. This is one reason why evil means should always be avoided. When an end seems to justify an evil means to that end, stop and remember that the end itself, which is a concrete existent, is always, to some degree, in doubt. A doubtful end cannot be used to justify an evil means. Furthermore, since the end follows the means and human life may cease abruptly at any moment, the evil means may exist and yet the good end may never exist. For at least these two reasons, a good end never justifies an evil means.

Working your way to a wise selection of a central Project may result in lasting tranquillity. Once you have made a defensible decision about the end, you can concentrate on the means and stop worrying about the end. For example, in my role as academic counselor to undergraduate students who have not yet selected a major course of study, I have frequently encountered students who are troubled about their selection. They realize that they must select a major and don't know how to do it. How could anyone select anything without knowing what it is *for*? If they lack a Project, how could they possibly justify any particular choice of means? On the other hand, if they have decided what they are trying to do with their lives, choosing a major that will get them closer to their goal is not usually difficult; if the end is known, why should it be difficult to select a major as a means to that end? The problem, of course, is that this means that the right way to select a major (or anything else) is first to figure out what you are trying to accomplish, what your Project is, what the meaning of your life is, and this is not easy. Because it is difficult, many people avoid it and the result is that they

199

muddle through life; they make even important decisions haphazardly. Isn't the alternative worth the effort? Why not do the hard thinking about your Project once and for all and then put that thinking behind you? Unless you are a philosopher, there is no need to keep rethinking it. You will then have a permanently available criterion for making decisions. This should greatly enhance your inner tranquillity by reducing your anxiety, your generalized fear that your life is meaningless. A student who selects a Project and a major as a means to it would then be free to concentrate on getting the most out of the courses that constitute that major.

What if, for example, you are a student who must select a major and you cannot seem to settle on a Project? Why not choose philosophy? A philosopher is a lover of wisdom. 'Lover' here means 'seeker after'; in other words, a philosopher is one who quests after wisdom. Someone who is wise lives well (lives excellently, leads the good life). So a philosopher is, essentially, a person who is seriously trying to live well. A decision to major in philosophy is a decision to seek the good life. What could be wrong with that? How could there be a better major than that?

Here are two examples of lives that satisfy my four criteria: a life of service and a life of inquiry.

A Life of Service. Let me give a specific example of a life of service. Suppose that there is a Catholic priest who dedicates his life to housing the homeless. Suppose that he works as an intermediary between the homeless in some urban ghetto and various private and public sponsors who are able and willing to provide money for sheltering the poor. It takes all his ingenuity to obtain a fairer distribution of housing.

Let us further imagine that this priest has a sound argument that concludes that it is just that the homeless should be housed. The chief idea behind this argument would be that there is enough wealth in the world to house all the poor without the rich sacrificing too much. Shelter is a good, and the just distribution of such goods is an intrinsically valuable end. This priest's Project is certainly challenging: the historical evidence may be used to suggest that he will never succeed in eliminating homelessness. And yet it is possible: it is not inconceivable that homelessness can be eliminated. Finally, it is easy to imagine that this Project provides this man with a continual source of lasting satisfaction. Year after year he feels good about what he is doing; he has no doubt that he is being useful to others.

It is important to note that it is not necessary to evaluate a person's motive(s) when evaluting his Project(s). In this case, the priest may be motivated to his life of service because he thinks of it as a life of worshipping God. But, even if it were false that God exists, the priest would still have performed a worthy service. Even if all the religious beliefs that motivated his Project were false, his life would not necessarily be meaningless.

If this is correct, questions about the supernatural may be irrelevant to questions about the good life. It is logically possible that supernatural beings exist. But, as far as I can see, there is no natural evidence that they exist. They are, at the very least, well hidden. Furthermore, there is no good reason to suppose, contrary to what many people believe, that questions about the good life depend for their answers upon the dictates or activities of supernatural beings. In other words, morality does not depend upon religion.[73] As in the case of our imagined priest, the quality of a person's life has

201

nothing to do with the correctness of that person's beliefs, if any, about the supernatural.

A Life of Inquiry. Suppose that there is a medical researcher who dedicates her life to trying to discover the cures for such scourges as AIDS or cancer or Alzheimer's disease. She has spent decades in the laboratory working diligently, after having spent years in medical school and post-graduate medical training.

Health is a good. This woman's Project is challenging in the sense that she is unlikely to run out of diseases to investigate. Her Project is possible: some diseases such as smallpox have been cured and there is every reason to expect continued success. Finally, her Project is likely to tax her creative powers to the utmost and to be a continual source of lasting satisfaction. Even if she herself fails to discover any additional cures, she may well succeed in eliminating various dead-ends, thus bringing the social Project of medical science a bit closer to its end.

Some might say that this is actually an example of a life of service, too. I shall not argue. The reason for this position is that, if successful, inquiry yields knowledge and knowledge is an abstract good. Medical knowledge can serve us all.

Comparing these two examples, is it better to try to house the homeless or to try to cure diseases? This question may be used to suggest a more general one. Given that there are different abstract goods and that the people who pursue them have different abilities, motivations, and interests, how, in principle, are potentially damaging conflicts between Projects to be avoided? I discuss this question in my final chapter.

10
Conflicts

Living is too important to do poorly. Living well is living the good life. But what exactly is the good life? The tale of our time is the tale of our disagreements.

What, we should each ask ourselves, should *my* reaction be to these disagreements? Should I conclude that the fundamental beliefs concerning the answers to questions of goodness concerning various concrete existents such as individuals and cultures are different or, worse, conflicting? Should I conclude that there is no rational way of solving disagreements about goodness? Should I conclude that what is good for one individual or culture is not good for another— even if the situations closely resemble each other?

Such conclusions do not directly follow from the fact of disagreement. Hence, my reaction should not be to adopt, without further thought, some variety of relativism. Roughly, relativism in this context is the idea that any person's opinions concerning the answers to questions about what is good are as good as their denial. It may be that some variety of relativism is correct; but, even if it is, its correctness does not directly follow from the fact that there is disagreement. The reason for this is the possibility that some opinions may be known to be true while conflicting opinions may only be (falsely) believed to be true.

For example, suppose that Alex and Betty disagree concerning the institution of private property. Betty, who is a communist, believes that private property is an evil institution that should therefore be abolished. Alex believes that being able to own things is a good and that, therefore, the institution of private property should not be abolished. Both Alex and Betty sincerely believe that their respective beliefs are true. Imagine that her central Project is to abolish the institution of private property and his is to increase its prevalence. Their Projects conflict and, if each attracted followers, war could be the result. Could either *know* that his or her belief is true? Is one belief justifiable? Or is neither justifiable? If, as a relativist would claim, neither is justifiable, then Alex's belief is as good as Betty's and vice-versa. (And each is equally bad!) If so, Alex and Betty may as well stop discussing and start fighting because no rational resolution is possible, because there is no truth about the correct answer here.

It is often possible to resolve disputes rationally by attaining either greater conceptual clarity or more factual information. As an example of the former, consider the issue of abortion. What are the ethically relevant characteristics of a human being? (I mention one answer below.) If we were clear about that, why couldn't we become clear about whether or not a fetus has those characteristics? As an example of the latter, consider a dispute about licensing a new landfill for the disposal of solid waste. What would be the consequences of putting a landfill on the proposed site? Knowing them would involve knowing a lot of relevant facts, for example, knowing how it was to be lined, knowing how it would affect the migration of ground water, knowing how it would affect local wildlife, knowing how much noise garbage trucks would make, knowing whether there were any alternatives (such as recycling programs) that would be more satisfactory in the long run, and so on. It would be foolish to make a decision in such a case without at least trying hard to learn the relevant facts, and learning the facts might well ameliorate the dispute.

The same might be true with respect to the issue concerning private property. Presumably, both Alex and Betty would be thinking of private property in the context of promoting (social, economic, and environmental) justice. If they were clear about the nature of justice, the dispute between them might reduce to the factual question of whether or not the institution of private property would be likely to result in an increase of justice. In other words, whether or not it is right to have the institution of private ownership might be an issue that is subject to rational resolution if we could attain both greater conceptual clarity about the nature of justice and more factual information. But what about disputes that survive the attainment of sufficient conceptual clarity and factual information?

Are rational resolutions of such value disagreements ever possible? Is there an ultimate difference between the realm of the normative, the realm of value, the realm of 'ought' (as in 'one ought not to steal' or 'one ought to be honest') and the realm of the descriptive, the realm of fact, the realm of 'is' (as in '7 plus 5 is 12' or 'it is the case that there are craters on the far side of the moon')? Is there a fundamental bifurcation between the realm of values and the realm of facts? If there is, then rational resolutions of value disagreements are impossible.[74] If there is not, then rational resolutions of value disagreements are possible; it would (in principle) be possible, for example, to improve either Alex's or Betty's understanding of the correct value of the institution of private property. In general, it would make sense to think of value judgments as being correct or incorrect, as being true or false.

This is a difficult issue. It is not easy to decide, and there have been impressively good thinkers on both sides of it. Of course, it is very easy to give an answer; what is difficult is justifying an answer. And an unjustified answer is worthless. The difficulty of giving a justified answer ought to increase our humility and decrease our confidence. There is no simple, quick justification for either answer to the question concerning the ultimate bifurcation between facts and values. Anyone alive to the issue is in the uncomfortable situation of being uncertain about its resolution. This is an excellent reason for being tolerant of opposing views.

It is an important issue. After all, what are all our disagreements about? You would not disagree with me about, say, the width of my desk; if it were important enough to us, we'd simply measure it. It is not such simple questions of fact that are important sources of disagreement. People disagree most vehemently about questions of value. As Plato points out in *Euthyphro*, it is these that cause discord, anger, hostility, and hatred.

So, disagreement exists concerning questions of value. (Of course, there is widespread agreement as well.) The fundamental question about value disagreements is whether there is an ultimate bifurcation between facts and values. This question is both difficult and important. Either values are facts or it is false that values are facts.

Neither alternative is initially palatable. If values are

facts, why is there so much disagreement? If there are 'value-facts', why don't we just determine them, when it is important enough to bother to do so, and resolve whatever issue is troubling us? On the other hand, if values are not facts, what are they? And how are we ever to manage to get along together without fighting if it is not even possible in principle to resolve our disagreements?

To live is to engage in various activities. But what makes one activity better than another? Can it be a fact that one activity is better than another? Or are there no such facts? This is the problem.

The problem will not solve itself; ignoring it will not make it go away. If it is to be solved at all, it will only be solved with concentrated intellectual effort.

But should *I* make the effort? Either I should or I shouldn't. At this point, neither alternative is justifiable. If it is false that values are facts, then no activity could ever be known to be better than another activity (for example, writing poetry could not be known to be better than murdering Jews). But is it false? If it is, then there is no (positive or negative) reason for engaging in any particular activity (including suicide). If value-facts do exist, then there may be a reason, for or against, engaging in any particular activity. (It does not automatically follow that there will be a reason because certain activities may be value-neutral.) If value-facts exist, there is nothing more important than determining their nature.

No one denies that serious disagreements about value exist. (Of course, trivial disagreements about value also exist, for example, whether or not a certain flavor of ice cream tastes better than another flavor.) One of two general explanations for this state of affairs must be correct; there is no third

207

alternative. Either value disagreements exist because there are no value-facts (and, so, people simply must make value judgments haphazardly as they go along) or value disagreements exist because, though value-facts exist, it is extremely difficult to determine their nature.

Which explanation is correct? I have argued in *The Fundamental Ideas* that value-facts exist even though it is extremely difficult to determine their nature. The position that I advocate may be correctly understood as an emendation of Plato's. Plato pointed out that there are certain immutable abstract existents and that they stand in certain immutable relations to one another. For example, 'two is a number' or 'crimson is a red' or, more generally, 'red is a color.' Of course, the words that we use to express such truths are invented— but the truths themselves are discovered. And, for example, 'crimson' is not the name of a wave-length (because there could be a blind physicist who knew perfectly well what wave-lengths are and who had never experienced colors). What would it be like for it to be false that crimson is a red? This is not merely someone's opinion; it is a fact that crimson is a red. Not everyone may recognize this fact. A person blind from birth is ignorant of it. But such a person's understanding is defective; it is not as if a blind person's knowledge of colors is somehow as good as a sighted person's.

Numbers and colors are not the most important kind of abstract existents; abstract goods are. Consider such truths as 'pleasure is a good' or 'knowledge is a good' or 'love is a good.' Aren't such truths also discovered? What would it be like for it to be false that, for example, pleasure is a good? (I discussed this in Chapter 4.) How could pleasure, *qua* pleasure, not be a good? It may be, then, that there is knowledge about abstract goods as well as knowledge about numbers and colors and other abstract entities.

Because abstract goods are properties, there may be a correlation between them and certain other properties of the concrete existents that exemplify them. Many philosophers (such as Plato, Aristotle, Plotinus, Aquinas, Descartes, Spinoza, Leibniz, and Locke) have thought that there could be a system of abstract goods. Though it would be better to call it the 'hierarchy' (or, even, 'cone' or 'pyramid') of goods (or 'perfections'), it is popularly known as the doctrine of the great chain of being.[75] As a contemporary illustration of this ancient doctrine, consider the following sketch of Panayot Butchvarov's theory of good and evil.[76] Let us consider it one step at a time.

1. Beings that are spatial (inanimate). Their corresponding abstract good is existence. Their corresponding abstract evil is nonexistence.

2. Beings that are living (animate). Their corresponding abstract good is health (including bodily integrity). Their corresponding abstract evil is ill-health (or disease including mutilation).

3. Beings that are sentient. Their corresponding abstract good is (bodily) pleasure. Their corresponding abstract evil is pain.

4. Beings that are rational (intelligent). Their corresponding abstract good is satisfaction of desires. Their corresponding abstract evil is dissatisfaction.

5. Beings that have intellect. Their corresponding abstract good is knowledge (or understanding as exemplified by philosophy, the sciences, and the arts). Their corresponding abstract evil is ignorance.

209

6. Beings that have will (volition). Their corresponding abstract good is fortitude (or firmness of will, which means following the dictates of the intellect instead of the promptings of bodily desire). Their corresponding abstract evil is weakness of will.

7. Beings that have sociality, in other words, relationships with other beings that possess intellect and will. Their corresponding abstract good is friendship (or brotherly love). Their corresponding abstract evil is friendlessness and enmity to friendship.

There are at least six initial points of interest to notice about this example. First, it is just an example. It needs to be worked out in detail, argued for, and defended in detail if it is even to count as a serious example. Butchvarov attempts to do that, but I mention it merely as a sample of what may be the right kind of theoretical position. Second, it is complicated. But that is surely a point in its favor: if the truth about what is good and evil were simple, everyone would already know it. Third, there may be more levels. Fourth, the beings that exemplify the properties characteristic of the three highest levels are of the same kind, namely, they are human beings. This, in fact, provides an account of human nature: "A human being occupies space, lives, is sentient, has desires, has the sort of intelligence deserving to be called intellect, is capable of volition, and is a member of a society of such beings".[77] These are supposed to be the ethically relevant characteristics of a human being (and not, for example, being a member of the biological species *Homo sapiens sapiens*). Fifth, the properties that are characteristic of the higher levels of beings are very complex, so it is not surprising that the corresponding abstract goods such as friendship and knowledge are also very complex. Sixth, the fact that (a kind of) love is at the top is in accordance with the kind of traditional thinking that claims that God is love.

Even if something like this position were the only plausible one, it would not follow that the sometimes difficult business of making daily decisions would necessarily be any easier. Knowledge of abstract goods is not the same as knowing which concrete existents are (indirectly) goods. For example, just because pleasure is an abstract good, it does not follow that every concrete instance of pleasure is unqualifiedly good; a particular concrete instance of pleasure may simultaneously exemplify an abstract evil. Insofar as it exemplified pleasure, it would be (indirectly) good, but insofar as it exemplified some abstract evil, it would be (indirectly) evil. But any ethical theory that failed to do justice to the complexity of many of our actual decisions would *obviously* be inadequate.

As Aristotle argued, a person with theoretical wisdom is not necessarily a person with practical wisdom. Part of what he may have had in mind concerns the development of that judgment that recognizes the applicability of theoretical knowledge. Again, it is one thing to know that crimson is a red and another thing to know that some particular piece of fabric is crimson. Since perception is fallible, since it is not a source of knowledge because incorrect judgments about perceptual objects are always possible, it is not possible to know that this fabric is crimson. Similarly, it is one thing to know that love is a good and another thing to know that some particular relationship is a loving relationship. It is as possible to be deceived about the true character of a particular relationship as it is to be deceived about the true color of a particular piece of fabric.

211

On the other hand, there is no decisive reason why one person cannot have both practical and theoretical wisdom. (There is a nondecisive reason: each takes a lot of time to develop and life is short.) It would certainly be good to have both practical and theoretical wisdom or, at least, a satisfactory degree of each. How might such a lofty position be attained? Possibly through a lot of book-learning and a lot of practical experience. I have tried in this book to distill some of the results of both sorts of experience.

Appendix

Your Physical Examination

I suggest reading the following description of those features typical of a state-of-the-art physical examination both before and after your own physical examination. Doing so will help you to get the most out of your exam and make the best evaluation of your physician's performance.[78] The order in which these features occur, either in the following list or in the physician's office, makes no difference.

a. *History.* Your physician should try to obtain from you a comprehensive health history. How do you feel? What diseases and operations have you had? What diseases have occurred in your family? What are your eating habits? What are your drinking habits? How much exercise do you get? Do you still smoke? Is your sex life satisfactory? What is the nature of your work environment? These are the kinds of questions that your physician should require you to answer, and you should answer all of them honestly and completely.

The reason for the history, which is often the most crucial part of the examination, is to provide your physician with information relevant to assessing the state of your health that cannot be provided as easily, if at all, by physical tests in the doctor's office. Your physician is trying to find out about those genetic and environmental features that may cause or predispose you toward certain diseases. For example, if you complain during the history of frequent headaches and memory loss and include in your description of your work environment the fact that you are constantly exposed to solvents, your physician may wish to investigate whether or not that exposure is causing your health to deteriorate. Or if you bring to your physician's attention during the history certain pains that you have been having lately, then upon investigation they may prove to be symptoms of some infectious disease or other and your physician may be able to cure that disease with antibiotics. Furthermore, a thorough history can help your physician to minimize the cost of the entire examination by eliminating the need for certain tests.

b. *Routine physical inspection.* Your physician (or, of course, his nurse or laboratory assistant) will want to make certain routine measurements such as height, weight, pulse rate, blood pressure, and, perhaps, percentage of body fat. Your physician will want to assess whether or not you are obese. Part of the purpose of these observations is to enable your physician to begin to assess the state of your fitness. If you are fit, you are more likely to be healthy than if you are unfit. So, if you are unfit and value your health, you may be able to improve your chances of being healthy by improving those habits that relate to health. For example, if you are an otherwise healthy but inactive young man with a waist measurement that exceeds forty inches, your physician should suggest a reducing diet and a program of regular, moderate exercise.

c. *Head and neck examination.* Your physician should want to determine if your head and neck are of normal size, whether or not there is any swelling in the lymph nodes, the condition of the pulse beat in the carotid arteries, and the condition of the thyroid gland. Abnormalities here could indicate a variety of health problems. For example, a nodule (mass of tissue) in the thyroid gland might be malignant; if so, early discovery could be the difference between life and death.

d. *Eye examination.* By looking carefully into your eyes your physician may detect indications of high blood pressure, diabetes, or brain tumors as well as of eye diseases. The reaction of your eyes to changes in light and distance should be checked. The lens of each eye should be evaluated for cataracts. Peripheral vision and eye pressure for those over 40 should be checked to see whether or not they are within normal limits. Without this examination, someone could suffer irreversible damage from glaucoma. Detected early, glaucoma may be easily treated with eye drops. But many people with glaucoma do not realize it themselves until it is too late—and the complete blindness that can result is unnecessary. This is a clear example of how it is possible to feel good and yet be in ill-health. A simple gross visual field examination by confrontation may give evidence of a brain tumor or stroke. And your vision should be checked to see if you ought to have glasses.

e. *Lymph node examination.* Your physician should want to palpate the lymph nodes throughout your body— under the arms and in the groin in addition to the neck. If one is unusually firm, it *may* be an early indicator of a potentially life-threatening condition. Depending upon the particular circumstances, a physician may want to have a firm lymph node removed and examined for malignancy (biopsied). The

215

system of lymph nodes is one of the body's defenses against infection and they are often enlarged or tender to the touch precisely because they are doing their job.

   f. *Chest examination.* Your physician will inspect, palpate and listen to your chest with a stethoscope. Abnormal sounds in the lungs can mean emphysema, asthma, or certain infectious diseases such as bronchitis or tuberculosis. Your physician can determine whether or not there is fluid in the chest, whether or not a lung is collapsed, and the extent to which the diaphragms can descend. Abnormal sounds or murmurs in the heart may be meaningless, although sometimes they may stimulate your physician to order further testing by means of a phono-cardiogram or an echocardiogram (ultrasonic) examination in order to determine, for example, the extent of an abnormality of a heart valve. Even these non-invasive techniques for evaluating the function of the heart are relatively expensive.

   A mammogram is a procedure for examining a woman's breasts for nodules. Experts currently disagree concerning the value of the procedure and, among those who value it, they disagree concerning its frequency. Most physicians would probably recommend yearly mammography for women over 50 with medium or large breasts. Women over 40, especially those with a family history of breast cancer and those with medium or large breasts, should at least discuss this aspect of the examination with their physicians. Facilities for doing mammograms are rather limited at the present time and, again, it is a fairly expensive procedure.

   g. *Abdominal examination.* Your physician will feel the front and sides of your abdomen in order to try to determine whether or not there are such features as an enlarged liver or spleen. If your physician suspects any difficulty (for example, gallstones), he may order an abdominal sonogram examination. This examination enables a physician to screen the liver, spleen, gall bladder, kidneys, and pancreas for abnormalities, to detect any unusual tissue masses, and to check the abdominal aorta for abnormalities. But the results of such a test may not be worth the expense. For example, the sonogram may detect an aneurysm of the abdominal aorta, but, at least in a patient with normal blood pressure, there may be little value in detecting it. It is possible to live with it for many years (and, even if it weren't, in this case medical treatment is probably superior to surgical treatment).

h. *Rectal examination.* This digital examination, which should include a prostate examination for men, is the only simple way to test the area for malignancies. Again, early detection of a small nodule may mean the difference between life and death. Your physician should also order a test in order to determine if there is any blood in the stool, which is a common early sign of cancer in the lower intestines. If you are over 40 and have not had one in two years, your physician should also order a sigmoidoscopic examination in order to help detect any polyps or early malignancies. A sigmoidoscopic examination that is conducted with a flexible sigmoidoscope may be superior to one that is conducted with a rigid sigmoidoscope. It would be wise to discuss these alternatives with your physician.

i. *Examination of bone structure and musculature.* Your physician should examine your bones and muscles for evidence of such abnormal musculoskeletal conditions as arthritis or fibromyocytis.

217

j. *Skin examination.* Your physician should carefully look at your skin to discover any skin lesions or minor malignancies, which are often caused by too much exposure to the sun. (If you ever notice a change in a mole, for example, if it grows darker or bleeds or seems to grow, you would be wise to bring it immediately to the attention of your physician.)

k. *Neurological system examination.* Your physician should make various kinds of tests to check your neurological system. He should, for example, test your reflexes. A difference in the reflex response of one ankle as compared to the other ankle might indicate a lower back disk problem, which is a problem of the peripheral nervous system. He should test your touch. He may wish to test your ability to sense pain (by pricking your skin with a pin). He may wish to test the strength in both arms—particularly if you are older and he suspects a small stroke problem. He should conduct or recommend further testing if he suspects a brain tumor, which is a problem of the central nervous system.

l. *Chemical profile of blood.* There are about two dozen laboratory tests that should be performed on a blood sample. Your physician should order a complete blood count (CBC). He will be looking for evidence of such disorders as anemia, leukemia, diabetes, cirrhosis of the liver and other liver diseases and abnormalities, kidney disease, calcium and phosphorus abnormalities, and any of the five different phenotypes of blood lipid abnormalities. For example, some researchers have argued that the ratio of total cholesterol to HDL cholesterol is important in predicting the likelihood of developing hardening of the arteries. Cooper thinks that, in men, the ratio ought to be less than 5.0 and should be less than 4.5 and that, in women, the ratio ought to be less than 4.0 and

218

should be less than 3.5. But for a physician to know this ratio he must order an HDL cholesterol test and such tests, though recommended by many researchers, are rather expensive. But, whichever tests your physician orders, he should look for lipid abnormalities, which can be corrected by diet, exercise, and, if needed, medication. Your overall cholesterol level is good if it is 200 or less; it is better if it is 180 or less. If you are not told what it is, ask. Your physician will also order a urinalysis.

m. *Hearing examination.* Your physician should check your hearing to see if you have any hearing problems. If any are detected, your physician should refer you to an otolaryngologist or, perhaps, to an audiologist.

n. *Pulmonary examination.* Your physician should conduct a spirometry test of the functioning of your lungs. This may detect asthma, bronchitis, emphysema, or other problems in the lungs or throat.

o. *Gastro-intestinal examination.* If your stool samples are positive for blood or if your physician suspects cancer or any other abnormalities, he may order a barium enema. If your physician suspects an ulcer and wishes to demonstrate it, he may order an endoscopy or an upper GI series or an X-ray examination.

p. *Chest X-ray.* If you are a smoker, an annual chest X-ray is extremely important. If you are a nonsmoker and have not had one in several years, your physician may order a chest X-ray to help determine whether your heart, lungs, and other organs are within normal size limits and without abnormalities.

q. *Treadmill stress test.* The results of this procedure can help a well-trained physician to evaluate your heart and cardiovascular fitness. Unfortunately, there are a number of problems with this test. First, it is expensive—several hundred dollars. Second, not all persons should be stress-tested. If you have certain kinds of chest pain, particularly if it is getting worse, you may be a person who should not take the test. On the other hand, your physician may want to give you the test because you have certain other kinds of chest pain. Third, not all physicians have the proper equipment in their offices to give a treadmill stress test. Fourth, not all physicians have had the training necessary to administer stress tests properly.

Nevertheless, a complete cardiac examination cannot be given without an exercise (stress) electrocardiogram (ECG). Your physician may determine that you do not need a complete cardiac examination if you are, say, a young, normally healthy woman. If you are an airplane pilot, however, your physician may believe that you need a complete cardiac examination. Discuss this matter with your physician. If the cost of the examination is of no concern to you, perhaps you will want to request a stress ECG. Or, together, you may determine that another sort of test (for example, a recovery ECG) is sufficient—particularly if you are without relevant symptoms. Even if there are relevant symptoms (for example, rhythm problems or if your heart is skipping beats or racing) another kind of test (for example, a Holter monitor, which monitors the heartbeat for 24 hours) might be preferable to a stress ECG. There are three different kinds of ECG tests.

i. If electrodes are taped to different parts of your torso and your physician reads an electrocardiograph that was taken when you were reclining on an examining table, you have received a resting ECG. But a resting ECG may miss many heart abnormalities and it is not a good way to measure cardiovascular fitness. Therefore, for decades physicians have preferred ECGs in which the patient is more active.

ii. If electrodes are taped to different parts of your torso, you are asked to step up and down on something repeatedly and rapidly, and you are then asked to rest while the electrocardiograph machine is switched on and the reading taken, you have received a recovery ECG. With these tests, it is necessary to take the reading during a rest because, if taken during the exercise, the vigorous jolting would interfere with the electric signals from the electrodes to the electrocardiograph machine. So this is not really an exercise ECG at all: it is a recovery ECG. One difficulty with a recovery ECG is that the precise rate of the exercise cannot be effectively monitored; a patient can simply speed up or slow down during the exercise. On the other hand, this is a safe test. And, since it is much less expensive than a stress ECG, the difference in their validity might not justify the additional expense of a stress ECG for certain patients.

iii. If electrodes are taped to different parts of your torso, you are asked to pump the pedals of a stationary bicycle, which is set at a certain resistance, and the electrocardiograph provides the reading during the exercise, you have received a stress ECG. During such a stress ECG the patient's heart and blood pressure are monitored with ease and the precise amount of exercise can be effectively monitored. So this test is superior to either a resting or a recovery ECG. But there are two difficulties with it. First, the legs of many patients are simply not conditioned to cycling and, second, even if a patient has strong, well-conditioned legs, only motivated patients need to push themselves to capacity. For these reasons, stress ECGs that use stationary bicycles are largely out of style. A motorized treadmill overcomes these problems.

If electrodes are taped to different parts of your torso, you are asked to walk and run on a motorized treadmill, and the electrocardiograph provides the reading during the exercise, you have received a stress ECG on a motorized treadmill. Unlike the pumping of a bicycle's pedals, the smooth, steady motion is a familiar motion—and one that does not interfere with the electric signals. And, since the speed and incline of the treadmill are controlled, the precise amount of exercise can be effectively monitored. This is not an ideal test, but it is an extremely good one in the hands of a well-trained physician. (The only definitive test currently available involves a certain mortality rate.)

If you are going to pay for a stress ECG on a motorized treadmill, you may as well ensure that you are getting your money's worth. After all, it is possible to own good equipment and not know how to use it correctly. When you are given the test, there are certain signs that you should look for. Are you allowed to hold on tightly to the bar during the test? If you are, conclude that the tester does not have adequate training; since holding on tightly to the bar will significantly decrease the energy that you expend, it will be impossible to quantify your level of fitness accurately. Are you exercised until you approach your predicated maximum heart rate? Cooper claims that your predicated maximum heart rate is simply 205 minus one-half your age. Compute it in advance. You should approach it quite closely in the test. If your test is stopped when you have only approached, say, 85 percent of your predicated maxi-mum heart rate, at least one-third of the abnormalities will be missed (according to Cooper).

r. *Special strength and flexibility testing.* If your physician suspects problems, he may order special tests to detect them. For example, Cooper gives the case of a patient in which lower back pain was the result of weak muscles at the back of the thighs (for which the cure was simply strengthening those muscles through a special set of corrective exercises).

s. *Psychological examination.* If you have never had one, your physician may want to have you take a psychological examination. This can help to indicate, for example, the amount of stress in your life and how you handle it. Stress may be an important risk factor in such maladies as cancer and heart disease. The Minnesota Multiphased Personality Inventory is a good, computer-scored exam. On the other hand, it may not be good enough in your particular case—or such a test may be unnecessarily expensive.

t. *Additional examinations.* Your physician ought to be able to recommend a good, local dentist if you do not have one. A complete dental examination by your dentist will include an examination of the appearance of your teeth and an evaluation of your bite. The appearance of one's teeth is an important part of one's self-image, and it is no longer necessary for one's teeth to fall out or to darken or to move around as one ages. A bad bite can cause headaches.

Your physician may perform (or order performed by an otolaryngologist) a laryngoscopic examination to see the vocal cords in an effort to detect cancer of the larynx.

If you are female, your physician should perform a Pap smear and a pelvic examination and direct you to a gynecologist if there are any problems.

Your physician may direct you to other specialists for assistance. Your physician may want to have a clinical psychologist or a psychiatrist administer and evaluate the psychological examination (if any). An ophthalmologist may be used for the eye examination; in fact, your physician may recommend that you visit an ophthalmologist regularly. Since such examinations add to the cost of the evaluation, they should be used only when needed. Of course, if your physician detects or suspects any abnormalities, he may, for example, call upon a surgeon to remove a cyst or suspicious nodule.

u. *Evaluation.* Your physician should want to meet with you personally to explain his findings. This is very important. What exactly is your condition? If there are any problems, are they curable? What is your health likely to be in the future? Are you, for example, likely to develop heart disease or cancer if you continue in your present habits? Is there anything you can do to improve the chances of your being healthy in the future?

This is a time for listening and learning. You are paying for the assessment and advice of an expert—so listen to it. If your physician gives you certain specific recommendations concerning eliminating poor physical habits or developing better physical habits of diet and exercise, those recommendations should, of course, override any of the general recommendations that I have given above in Chapters 3, 4, and 5.

It is during the evaluation that you should want to find out why, if your physician has failed to perform any of the tests that I have mentioned, you have not received them. There may be a satisfactory answer. Perhaps, for someone of your age and in your general condition a particular test may likely be only an unnecessary expense. On the other hand, it may be that you are not receiving a comprehensive enough

224

examination. If you decide that that is the case, then you should get another physician. Your physician works for you—not the other way around. But it is wise to be diplomatic here. If you do not have a license to practice medicine, do not expect to tell a licensed physician how to do it properly without some negative reaction. Even if you happen to be correct, it is better to suggest that your examination be a bit more comprehensive than to be so aggressive about it that you alienate the expert whom you have chosen.

Notes

Chapter 1

1. Franklin, p. 159. (Complete information on the works cited in these notes is to be found in the bibliography.)
2. Franklin, pp. 122–23.
3. Franklin. p.123.

Chapter 2

4. See my *The Fundamental Ideas*, Chapter 13.
5. Descartes, Sixth Meditation.
6. For the distinction between knowledge and rational belief, see Chapter 3 in *The Fundamental Ideas*.
7. For more on this topic, see Donald F. Tapley, M.D., et al., Chapter 2.
8. These are Cooper's recommendations from *The Aerobics Program for Total Well-Being*, p. 220.

Chapter 3

9. See Chapter 9.
10. Quoted in *JAMA* 1984, vol. 252, #20, 2803–04.
11. Two good starting points for additional reading about this are: Baruch A. Brody, ed., *Readings in the Philosophy of Religion* and William J. Wainwright, *Philosophy of Religion*.
12. An initial defense of this controversial claim can be found in Chapter 6 of *The Fundamental Ideas*. A good starting point for additional reading is Baruch A. Brody, ed., *Readings in the Philosophy of Science*.
13. For an introductory discussion of the nature of understanding, see Chapter 2 in *The Fundamental Ideas*.
14. James, I, 123.
15. James, I, 123.
16. James, I, 126.

Chapter 4

17. Plato, 499.
18. Plato, 503–04.
19. An excellent, short introductory work is Frankena's *Ethics*. Butchvarov's *Skepticism in Ethics* is an excellent, difficult, stimulating, comprehensive contemporary theory that I have relied on heavily in the following section.
20. Plato, 509. Discussions of his theory of 'forms' and doctrine of 'participation' are scattered throughout his dialogues.
21. The properties are really being pleasurable, being beau-

tiful, and being known, However, there is no serious reason to be so pedantic.

22. See Frankena, Chapter 5.

23. *Jane Brody's Good Food Book*, pp. 554–610. Her 'high-protein three-grained bread' is a favorite at our home.

24. I am 6'2" tall with what an Army physician once classified as a 'heavy' build.

25. Cooper, *The Aerobics Program for Total Well-Being*, p. 71.

26. I did not avoid beer drinking in college and, while I was in the army, I wanted to make sure that my social life was not becoming too centered around drinking instead of the other way around. So I didn't drink a drop of any alcoholic beverage for over a year. It is a sensible step to take if you think you might have a problem.

27. These are all Cooper's recommendations. Cooper, *The Aerobics Program for Total Well-Being*, p. 73.

Chapter 5

28. See Butchvarov, Chapter 8.

29. Cf. Cooper, *The Aerobics Program for Total Well-Being*, 108–114.

30. Some may want to know what that experience is. In high school, I played JV basketball, lettered as a quarterback in varsity football, and was captain of a city-league hockey team. I discovered that I lacked the speed and quickness to be a really good athlete. For example, when the first-string quarterback went down with an injury, I stepped in—and the coach had to eliminate a

whole series of plays from our game plans because I was too slow to run them. (They were option plays, but by the time I could get out to option on the defensive end the entire line of scrimmage had usually collapsed!) On the ice I was a defensive defensemen. I ruled out bodybuilding even though I was interested in it because I thought (probably mistakenly) that it would cause osteoarthritis. (At least there I had some potential: I happen to be the same height as Arnold Schwarzenegger!) I did little exercise as an undergraduate or graduate student. When I took a teaching position, I went back to playing (full body-contact) hockey after a 15-year layoff. I ran to get in shape for hockey. I played for eight seasons in my thirties in a Rochester, New York, adult hockey league. (I was fortunate enough to be on a good team. During that time we finished first during the regular season four times and won the play-offs three times.) I was alternate captain for two seasons and captain for two seasons. Today, I still run and play senior (over 30, no deliberate body-checking) hockey.

31. Some authorities deny the distinction between healthy sweat and nervous perspiration—which probably means that it depends upon the individual.

32. Bradley, pp. 90–91.

33. Cooper, *The Aerobics Program for Total Well-Being*, p. 170.

34. And, though I have broken a few bones playing hockey, I have only infrequently suffered muscle pulls or strains.

35. *The Elder Edda*, pp. 40–41.

Chapter 6

36. For a brief, general account of understanding, see my *The Fundamental Ideas*, Chapter 2. I am assuming here that improving the student's understanding is the essential aim of teaching. I recognize, however, that a teacher can also intend to teach, for example, a skill or an attitude.

37. Plato, 150. Today of course, the analogy would be to an obstetrician.

38. Plato, *Meno*, 86b–c, and *Republic*.

39. Some readers may want to know what my own educational background is. I attended public elementary school. Though I attended public high school for three years, I spent my senior year at a private prep school, Blair Academy. After graduation, I spent four years as an undergraduate (pre-professional) philosophy major at Syracuse University. I later attended The University of Iowa where I received an M.A. and a Ph.D. in philosophy. Since then I have been a professor of philosophy at S.U.N.Y. Geneseo. I have taught undergraduate humanities courses (ones in literature, history, and philosophy) as well as philosophy courses.

40. Thucydides, p. 48.

Chapter 7

41. Marx, p. 160. It is not my intention to make a general endorsement of Marxism; rather, I am simply drawing

attention to one good point that Marx made about the quality of life.

42. I know this because I have worked first shift as a professor, army officer, parole officer for juvenile delinquents, and air hammer operator; I have worked second shift as a fork lift operator, night watchman, laborer (moving inventory), and bartender; and I have worked third shift as a medical orderly and night clerk/auditor in a motel.

43. Townsend, p. 175.

44. Townsend, p. 107.

45. Molloy, p. 12. He frequently considers women's clothes in his syndicated newpaper column.

46. Confucius, p. 37.

47. Townsend, p. 211.

Chapter 8

48. It may be relevant to the discussion in the next chapter. Suppose, for example, that you are a Marxist who wants to change our economic system and that you think that such a change is so important that you have made it your Project. Still, you will be more likely to achieve success if you first attain financial independence.

49. I thank David Ramsay Steele for the following two formulations.

50. Hume, Book I, Part III.

51. For more on such ideas, see the first two chapters of Allen's *Creating Wealth*.

52. Daigh, p. 3.

53. Daigh, p. 7.
54. Spinoza, p. 400. Or "all that is excellent and eminent is as difficult as it is rare (infrequent)."
55. 1095b.
56. Cf. Allen, *Creating Wealth*, Chapter 3.

Chapter 9

57. Leo Tolstoy, selection from 'A Confession', quoted from Beauchamp and Perlin's *Ethical Issues in Death and Dying*, p. 322.
58. See Chapter 1, *The Fundamental Ideas*.
59. See Descartes, the First Meditation.
60. See Kurt Baier's essay in the volume edited by Steven Saunders and David R. Cheney.
61. See Lovejoy.
62. Nietzsche, *Basic Writings*, p. 417. Kaufmann draws the obvious conclusion: "We are in no position to tell who among our contemporaries is great". (Note 33).
63. Dostoevsky, *Crime and Punishment*, p. 344. Incidentally, recall how Dostoevsky has Porfiry point out another difficulty with the distinction of rank among men, namely, our tendency always to assume that we ourselves are of the first rank (p. 225).
64. Micah, 6:8. *The New English Bible*. I thank Bill Edgar and Walt Soffer for this reference.
65. 1094al.
66. 1094a17–21.
67. Cf. Frankena, pp. 87–88.
68. 1097b–1098a.

69. 1095b.
70. See, for example, Taylor.
71. Camus, p. 40.
72. 1098a.
73. See *The Fundamental Ideas*, esp. pp. 143–44 and 169–172, and Plato 10a–11b.

Chapter 10

74. I am not here counting a decision by, for example, majority vote for a rational resolution; there are many such decision procedures. The question is whether or not there can be rational agreement.
75. See Lovejoy.
76. Butchvarov, Chapter 5.
77. Butchvarov, pp. 86–87.

Appendix

78. Another popular guide here is Chapter 12 of Kenneth H. Cooper M.D., M.P.H. (Master of Public Health), *The Aerobics Program for Total Well-Being*. In general, Cooper's recommended examination would be very expensive; not all the tests that he recommends are routinely necessary for everyone.

Bibliography

'*JAMA*' abbreviates '*The Journal of the American Medical Association.*'

'*NEJMAG*' abbreviates '*The New England Journal of Medicine.*'

Allen, Robert G. *Creating Wealth*. New York: Simon and Schuster, 1983.

————. *Nothing Down*. New York: Simon and Schuster, 1980.

Andersen, M.D., Teis, et al. 'Randomized Trial of Diet and Gastroplasty Compared With Diet Alone in Morbid Obesity'. *NEJMAG*, 310, 6, 352–56.

Angell, M.D., Marcia. 'Disease as a Reflection of the Psyche'. *NEJMAG*, 312, 24, 1570–72.

Anonymous. *The Elder Edda: A Selection*. Trans. Paul B. Taylor and W. H. Auden. New York: Vintage, 1967.

Appelbaum, Judith, and Evans, Nancy. *How To Get Happily Published*. New York: Harper and Row, 1978.

235

Aristotle. *The Complete Works of Aristotle.* Ed., Jonathan Barnes. Princeton, N.J.: Princeton University Press, 1984.

Arntzenius, M.D., Alexander C., et al. 'Diet, Lipoproteins, and the Progression of Coronary Atherosclerosis: The Leiden Intervention Trail.' *NEJMAG*, 312, 13, 805–811.

Beauchamp, Tom L., and Perlin, Seymour, eds. *Ethical Issues in Death and Dying.* Englewood Cliffs, N.J.: Prentice-Hall, 1978.

Belgan, M.D., John R., et al. 'Council Report: Exercise Programs for the Elderly'. *JAMA*, 252, 4, 544–46.

Bergan, M.D., John J. 'Abdominal Aortic Aneurysm'. *JAMA*, 253, 21, 3166.

Black, M.D., Donald W. 'Laughter'. *JAMA*, 252, 21, 2995-98.

Blankenhorn, M.D., David H. 'Two New Diet-Heart Studies'. *NEJMAG*, 312, 13, 851–53.

Blair, P. E. D., Steven N., et al. 'Physical Fitness and Incidence of Hypertension in Healthy Normotensive Men and Women'. *JAMA*, 252, 4, 487–490.

Bloch, H.I. Sonny, and Lichtenstein, Grace. *Inside Real Estate.* N.Y.: Grove Weidenfeld, 1987.

Bradford, Dennis E. *The Fundamental Ideas.* St. Louis, MO: Warren H. Green, 1986.

Bradley, Bill. *Life on the Run.* New York: Bantam, 1976.

Brean, Herbert. *How to Stop Smoking.* New York: Pocket, 1951.

Brody, ed., Baruch A. *Readings in the Philosophy of Religion.* Englewood Cliffs, N.J.: Prentice-Hall, 1974.

————. *Readings in the Philosophy of Science.* Englewood Cliffs, N.J.: Prentice-Hall, 1970.

236

Brody, Jane. *Jane Brody's Good Food Book: Living the High-Carbohydrate Way.* New York: Norton, 1985.

Brown, Rita Mae. *Starting From Scratch: A Different Kind of Writers' Manual.* New York: Bantam, 1988.

Bullen, Sc. D., Beverly A., et al. 'Induction of Menstrual Disorders By Strenuous Exercise in Untrained Women'. *NEJMAG*, 312, 21, 1349–353.

Butchvarov, Panayot. *Skepticism in Ethics.* Bloomington and Indianapolis: Indiana University Press, 1989.

Cahn, Steven M., ed. *Classics of Western Philosophy.* 2nd ed. Indianapolis: Hackett, 1985.

Callaway, M.D., C. Wayne. 'Nutrition'. *JAMA*, 252, 16, 2283–86.

Camus, Albert. *The Myth of Sisyphus and Other Essays.* New York: Vintage, 1955.

Cantwell, M.D., John D. 'Hygiene of Baths After Exercise'. *JAMA*, 252, 3, 429.

Carlson, Lars A. 'Serum Triglycerides—An Independent Risk Factor For Myocardial Infarction But Not for Angina Pectoris'. *NEJMAG*, 312, 17, 1127.

Cassileth, Ph.D., Barrie R., et al. 'Psychosocial Status in Chronic Illness: A Comparative Analysis of Six Diagnostic Groups'. *NEJMAG*, 311, 8, 506–511.

Chodak, M.D., Gerald W., and Schoenberg, M.D., Harry W. 'Early Detection of Prostate Cancer by Routine Screening'. *JAMA*, 252, 23, 3261–64.

Claiborne, Craig, with Franey, Pierre. *Craig Clairborne's Gourmet Diet.* New York: Ballantine, 1980.

Conn, M.D., Rex B., et al. 'Identifying Costs of Medical Care:

An Essential Step in Allocating Resources'. *JAMA*, 253, 11, 1586–89.

Cook, Wade B. *How to Build a Real Estate Money Machine*. Salt Lake City, UT: National Institute of Financial Planning, 1983.

Cooper, M.D., M.P.H., Kenneth H. *Controlling Cholesterol*. New York: Bantam, 1988.

Cooper, M.D., M.P.H., Kenneth H. *The Aerobics Program for Total Well-Being*. New York: Bantam, 1982.

Coser, Lewis A., Kadushin, Charles, and Powell, Walter W. *Books: The Culture and Commerce of Publishing*. New York: Basic, 1982.

Council of Scientific Affairs. 'Early Detection of Breast Cancer'. *JAMA*, 252, 21, 3008–011.

Council of Scientific Affairs. 'Exercise Programs for the Elderly'. *JAMA*, 252, 4, 544-46.

Dardik, M.D., F.A.C.S., Irving, and Waitley, Ph.D., Denis. *Quantum Fitness*. New York: Simon and Schuster, 1984.

Debusk, M.D., Robert F. 'Exercise Test Supervision by Nonphysicians'. *JAMA*, 252, 22, 3182.

Descartes, René. *Meditations on First Philosophy in which the Existence of God and the Distinction of the Soul from the Body are Demonstrated*. Indianapolis: Hackett, 1979. Donald A. Cress, tr.

Dimnet, Ernest. *The Art of Thinking*. New York: Simon and Schuster, 1928.

Dimsdale, M.D., Joel E. 'Postexercise Peril'. *JAMA*, 251, 6, 630–32.

Donner, M.D., Howard J. 'Out in the Cold.' *Emergency Medicine*, 31–34.

Dostoevsky, Feodor. *Crime and Punishment.* Trans. Jessie Coulson. New York: Norton, 1975.

Eaton, M.D., S. Boyd, and Konner, Ph.D., Melvin. 'Paleolithic Nutrition: A Consideration of Its Nature and Current Implications'. *NEJMAG*, 312, 5, 283–89.

Ernst, M.D., E. 'Changes in Blood Rheology Produced by Exercise'. *JAMA*, 253, 20, 2962–63.

Ewing, M.D., John A. 'Detecting Alcoholism: The Cage Questionaire'. *JAMA*, 252, 14, 1905–07.

Fatteh, Faiz. 'Alcohol is Dangerous to Your Health'. *JAMA*, 253, 20, 2959–960.

Fielding, M.D., M.P.H., Jonathon E. 'Smoking: Health Effects and Control' (First of Two Parts). *NEJMAG*, 313, 8, 491–98.

———. 'Smoking: Health Effects and Control', (Second of Two Parts). *NEJMAG*, 313, 9, 555–561.

Forgey, M.D., William. *Wilderness Medicine.* Pittsboro, IN: Indiana Camp Supply, 1979.

Frankena, William K. *Ethics.* 2nd ed. Englewood Cliffs, N.J.: Prentice-Hall, 1973.

Frankena, William K. and John T. Granrose, eds. *Introductory Readings in Ethics.* Englewood Cliffs, N.J.: Prentice-Hall, 1974.

Franklin, Benjamin. *The Autobiography of Benjamin Franklin.* Norwalk, Conn.: Heritage, 1979.

Froelicher, M.D., Victor, et al. 'A Randomized Trial of Exercise

Training in Patients With Coronary Heart Disease'. *JAMA*, 252, 10, 1291–97.

Gamow, George. 'The Evolutionary Universe.' *Scientific American* (September 1956).

Glomset, M.D., John A. 'Fish, Fatty Acids, and Human Health'. *NEJMAG*, 312, 19, 1253–54.

Glubetich, Dave. *The Monopoly Game: The 'How To' Book of Making Big Money With Rental Homes.* 4th ed. Pleasant Hill, CA: Impact, 1981

Goldberg, M.D., Linn, et al., 'Changes in Lipid and Lipoprotein Levels After Weight Training'. *JAMA*, 252, 4, 504-06.

Goldman, M.D., Peter, 'Coffee and Health: What's Brewing?' *NEJMAG*, 310, 12, 783–85.

Gott, Gunn, Schramm, Tinsley. 'Will the Universe Expand Forever?' *Scientific American* (March 1976).

Grundy, M.D., Ph.D., Scott M. et al. 'Consensus Conference: Treatment of Hypertriglyceridemia'. *JAMA*, 251, 9, 1196–1200.

Gunchow, Ph.D., Harvey W., et al. 'Alcohol, Nutrient Intake, and Hypertension in US Adults'. *JAMA*, 253, 11, 1567–570.

Haggerty, M.D., Robert J. 'The Limits of Medical Care'. *NEJMAG*, 313, 6, 383–84.

Hall, Craig. *The Real Estate Turnaround.* Englewood Cliffs, N.J.: Prentice Hall, 1978.

Harlan, M.D., William R., and Stross, M.D., Jeoffrey. 'An Educational View of a National Initiative to Lower Plasma Lipid Levels'. *JAMA*, 253, 14, 2087–090.

Hartz, M.D., Ph.D., Arthur, J., et al. 'The Association of Smoking With Cardiomyopathy *NEJMAG*, 311, 19, 1201-06.

Haskell, Ph.D., William L., et al. 'The Effect of Cessation and Resumption of Moderate Alcohol Intake on Serum High-Density-Lipoprotein Subfractions'. *NEJMAG*, 310, 13, 805–810.

Havey, M.D., Robert J. 'Classic Case'. *JAMA*, 252, 20, 2886.

Heidegger, Martin. *Being and Time*. Trans. John Macquarrie and Edward Robinson. New York: Harper and Row, 1962.

Helzer, M.D., John E., et al. 'The Extent of Long-Term Moderate Drinking Among Alcoholics Discharged from Medical and Psychiatric Treament Facilities'. *NEJMAG*, 312, 26, 1678 1682.

Herbert, M.D., Peter N., et al. 'High-Density Lipoprotein Metabolism in Runners and Sedentary Men'. *JAMA*, 252, 8, 1034–37.

Herzog, M.D., David B., and Copeland, M.D., Paul M. 'Eating Disorders'. *NEJMAG*, 313, 5, 295, 303.

Hick, John. *Philosophy of Religion*. Englewood Cliffs, N.J.: Prentice-Hall, 1963.

Hjalmarson, Ph.D., Agneta I.M. 'Effect of Nicotine Chewing Gum in Smoking Cessation'. *JAMA*, 252, 20, 2835–38.

Hubley-Kozey, M.Sc., Cheryl L., and Stanish, M.D., William D. 'Can Stretching Prevent Athletic Injuries?' *The Journal of Musculoskeletal Medicine*. March 1990. 21–31.

Hughes, M.D., John R. and Miller, M.S., Stephen A. 'Nicotine Gum to Help Stop Smoking'. *JAMA*, 252, 20, 2855-58.

Hume, David. *A Treatise of Human Nature*. L. A. Selby-Bigge, ed. 2nd ed. by P.H. Nidditch. Oxford: Clarendon, 1978.

Huston, M.D., Tim P., et al. 'The Athletic Heart Syndrome'. *NEJMAG*, 313, 1, 24-32.

Irvine, M.D., Patrick. 'Sounding Board: The Attending at the Funeral'. *NEJMAG*, 312, 26, 1704–05.

Jajich, M.P.H., Cindy L., et al. 'Smoking and Coronary Heart Disease Mortality in the Elderly'. *JAMA*, 252, 20, 2831–34.

James, William. *The Principles of Psychology.* 1,4. New York: Dover, 1950. (This is a reprint of the 1890 edition.)

King, M.D., Lester S. '"Hey, You!" and Other Forms of Address' *JAMA*, 254, 2, 266–67.

Klemke, E.D., ed. *The Meaning of Life.* New York: Oxford, 1981.

Kromhout, Ph.D., M.P.H., Daan, et al. 'The Inverse Relation Between Fish Consumption and 20-year Mortality From Coronary Heart Disease'. *NEJMAG*, 312, 19, 1205-09.

Kushi, Sc.D., Lawrence, H., et al. 'Diet and 20-year Mortality From Coronary Heart Disease: The Ireland-Boston Diet-Heart Study' *NEJMAG*, 312, 13, 811-18.

Landry, Ph.D., Fernand, et al. 'Cardiac Dimension Changes With Endurance Training'. *JAMA*, 254, 1, 77-80.

Larsson, B., et al. 'Health and Aging Characteristics of Highly Physically Active 65-year-old Men'. *European Heart Journal*, 5 (Supplement E), 31–35.

Laslett, M.D., Lawrence J., and Amsterdam, M.D., Ezra A. 'Management of the Asymptomatic Patient With an Abnormal Exercise ECG'. *JAMA*, 252, 13, 1744–46.

Lemmon, John. 'Moral Dilemmas'. Reprinted in William K. Frankena and John T. Granrose, eds., *Introductory Read-*

ings in Ethics (Englewood Cliffs, N.J.: Prentice-Hall, 1974), pp. 17–28.

Levy, M.D., Robert I. 'High HDL Cholesterol and Elevated Total Serum Cholesterol Levels'. *JAMA*, 254, 4, 546–47.

Lieber, M.D., Charles S. 'To Drink (Moderately) or Not to Drink?' *NEJMAG*, 310, 13, 846–48.

Lipid Research Clinics Program. 'The Lipid Research Clinics Coronary Primary Prevention Trial Results: II. The Relationship of Reduction in Incidence of Coronary Heart Disease to Cholesterol Lowering'. *JAMA*, 254, 7, 919–924.

Logan, M.D., Wende W., and Love, M.D., Susan M., 'Fibrocystic Breast Disease and Annual Mammagraphy'. *JAMA*, 253, 22, 3315–16.

Lovejoy, Arthur O. *The Great Chain of Being.* New York: Harper and Row, 1936.

Lowry, Albert J. *How to Manage Real Eestate Successfully in Your Spare Time.* New York: Simon and Schuster, 1977.

———. *How You Can Become Financially Idependent by Investing in Real Estate.* Revised Edition. New York: Simon and Schuster, 1982.

Lundberg, M.D., George D. 'Ethyl Alcohol—Ancient Plaque and Modern Poison'. *JAMA*, 252, 14, 1911–12.

MacFarlane, M.B.B.S., Ph.D., Donald and York, M.D., Elihu. 'Diet and Coronary Heart Disease'. *NEJMAG*, 313, 2, 118–19.

MacIntyre, Alasdair. *A Short History of Ethics.* New York: Macmillan, 1966.

Marwick, Charles. 'Changing Climate Seen in Efforts to Tell

Public About Smoking Health'. *JAMA*, 252, 20, 2797-99.

———. 'Effects of "Passive Smoking" Lead Nonsmokers to Step Up Campaign'. *JAMA*, 253, 20, 2937–39.

———. 'Many Physicians Following Own Advice About Not Smoking'. *JAMA*, 252, 20, 2804.

———. 'Wheelchair Calisthenics Keep Patients Fit'. *JAMA*, 251, 3, 303.

Marx, Karl. *The Marx-Engels Reader.* Robert C. Tucker, ed., Second Edition. New York: Norton, 1978.

Matsukura, M.D., Shigeru, et al. 'Effects of Environmental Tobacco Smoke On Urinary Cotinine Excretion in Non-smokers'. *NEJMAG*, 311, 13, 828–832.

McGill, V. J. *The Idea of Happiness.* New York: Praeger, 1967.

McManus, M.D., Ph.D., Bruce M., et al. '"Normal" Blood Cholesterol Levels'. *NEJMAG*, 312, 1, 51–52.

McNabb, M.D., McKendrea E. 'Nicotine Gum Addiction?' *JAMA*, 252, 20, 2890.

Miller, Peter G., and Bregman, Douglas M. *The Common-Sense Guide to Successful Real Estate Negotiation.* New York: Harper and Row, 1987.

Mirkin, M.D., Gabe, and Shangold, M.D., Mona. 'Muscle Cramps During Exercise'. *JAMA*, 253, 11, 1634.

———. Review of Bob Goldman, et al. *Death in the Locker Room: Steroids and Sports. JAMA*, 252, 19, 2771.

Molloy, John T. *Dress for Success.* New York: Warner, 1975.

Moore, Alma Chesnut. *How to Clean Everything.* New York: Simon and Schuster, 1977.

Most, M.D., Harry. 'Current Concepts: Treatment of Parasitic

Infections of Travelers and Immigrants.' *NEJMAG*, 311, 14, 874–77.

Name Withheld. 'Drunks and Denial.' *JAMA*, 252, 14, 1869.

Neff, Glenda Tennant, ed. *1990 Writer's Market*. Cincinnati: Writer's Digest, 1989.

Nickerson, William. *How I Turned $1,000 into Five Million in Real Estate— In My Spare Time*. Revised Edition. New York: Simon and Schuster, 1980.

Nietzsche, Friedrich. *Basic Writings of Nietzsche*. Ed. and trans. Walter Kaufmann. New York: Modern Library (Random House), 1968.

Niven, M.D., Robert G. 'Alcoholism: A Problem in Perspective'. *JAMA*, 252, 14, 1912–14.

O'Donoghue, Don H. *Treatment of Injuries to Athletes*. Philadelphia: Saunders, 1984.

Orlandi, Ph.D., M.P.H., Mario A. 'Smoking Clinics: Do They Work?' *JAMA*, 253, 20, 3017.

Paffenbarger, Jr., M.D., D.P.H., Ralph S., et al. 'A Natural History of Athleticism and Cardiovascular Health'. *JAMA*, 252, 4, 491–95.

Pariza, Ph.D., Michael W. 'A Perspective on Diet, Nutrition, and Cancer'. *JAMA*, 251, 11, 1455–58.

Pell, Ph.D., Sidney, and Fayerweather, M.P.H., William E 'Trends in the Incidence of Myocardial Infarction and in Associated Mortality and Morbidity in a Large Employed Population, 1957–1983'. *NEJMAG*, 312, 16, 1005–011.

Petersen's Home Repair and Maintenance Guide. Los Angeles: Petersen, 1977.

245

Plato. *The Collected Dialogues of Plato Including the Letters*. Edith Hamilton and Huntington Cairns, eds. Princeton N.J.: Princeton University Press, 1961.

Pollin, M.D., William. 'The Role of the Addictive Process as a Key Step in Causation of All Tobacco-Related Diseases'. *JAMA*, 252, 20, 2874.

Popkin, Richard H. *The History of Skepticism from Erasmus to Descartes*. Revised Edition. New York: Harper and Row, 1964.

Pritikin, Nathan, with McGrady, Jr., Patrick, M. *The Pritikin Program for Diet for Exercise*. New York: Bantam, 1979.

Radovsky, M.D., Saul S. 'Occasional Notes: Bearing the News'. *NEJMAG*, 313, 9, 586, 588.

Rahimtoola, M.D., Shanbudin H. 'Cholesterol and Coronary Heart Disease: A Perspective'. *JAMA*, 253, 14, 2094–95.

Renington, M.D., Patrick L. 'Current Smoking Trends in the United States: The 1981–1983 Behavioral Risk Factor Survey'. *JAMA*, 253, 20, 2970–74.

Renshaw, M.D., Doneena C. 'Sexology'. *JAMA*, 252, 16, 2291–95.

Reuler, M.D., James B. et al. 'Adult Scurvy'. *JAMA*, 253, 6, 805–07.

Rifkind, M.D., F.R.C.P., Basil M., et al. Letters and Replies on 'Lipid Research Clinics Program'. *JAMA*, 252, 18, 2545–48.

Robinson, Leigh. *Landlording*. Richmond, CA: ExPress, 1980.

Rogers, Ph.D., Robert L. 'Abstention from Cigarette Smoking Improves Cerebral Perfusion Among Early Chronic Smokers'. *JAMA*, 253, 20, 2970–74.

Rosenberg, Sc.D., Lynn, et al. 'Breast Cancer and Cigarette Smoking'. *NEJMAG*, 310, 2, 92–94.

Rosenberg, Sc.D., Lynn, et al. 'Myocardial Infarction and Cigarette Smoking in Women Younger than 50 Years of Age'. *JAMA*, 253, 20, 2965–69.

Sandage, Allan R. 'The Red–Shift'. *Scientific American* (September 1956).

Sanders, Steven, and Cheney, David R., eds. *The Meaning of Life: Questions, Answers and Analysis*. Englewood Cliffs, N.J.: Prentice–Hall, 1980.

Sawka, Ph.D., Michael N., et al. 'Influence of Hydration Level and Body Fluids on Exercise Performance in the Heat'. *JAMA*, 252, 9, 1165–69.

Saxbe, M.D., M.P.H., William B. 'Exercise and Sudden Cardiac Death'. *NEJMAG*, 312, 3, 183–84.

Schneider, M.D., Edward L., and Reed, Jr., B.S., John D. 'Life Extension'. *NEJMAG*, 312, 18, 1159–168.

Sheehan, M.D., George A. *Dr. Sheenan on Running*. New York: Bantam, 1975.

Simon, M.D., Harvey B. 'The Immunology of Exercise'. *JAMA*, 252, 19, 2735–38.

Siscovick, M.D., David S., et al. 'The Incidence of Primary Cardiac Arrest During Vigorous Exercise'. *NEJMAG*, 311, 14, 874–77.

Somers, Anne R. 'Sounding Board'. *NEJMAG*, 311, 13, 853-56.

Spinoza. *Spinoza: Selections*. Ed. John Wild. New York: Charles Scribner's Sons, 1930.

Stamler, M.D., Jeremiah. 'Coronary Heart Disease: Doing the "Right Things"'. *NEJMAG*, 312, 16, 1053–55.

Steinberg, M.D., Ph.D., Daniel, et al. 'Consensus Conference: Lowering Blood Cholesterol to Prevent Heart Disease'. *JAMA*, 253, 14, 2080–86.

Steinfeld, M.D., Jesse L. "Smoking and Lung Cancer." JAMA, 253, 20, 2995–2997.

Tapley, M.D., Donald F., et. al., Medical Editors. *The Columbia Univeristy College of Physicians and Surgeons Complete Home Medical Guide*. Mt. Vernon, N.Y.: Consumers Union, 1985.

Taylor, Richard. 'Time and Life's Meaning'. *The Review of Metaphysics*. XL. 4. 675–686.

Thompson, M.D., Paul D. and Mitchell, M.D., Jere H. 'Exercise and Sudden Cardiac Death'. *NEJMAG*, 311, 14, 914–15.

Thucydides. *History of the Peloponnesian War*. Trans. Rex Warner. Baltimore: Penguin, 1954.

Thurow, Lester Carl. 'Sounding Board: Learning To Say "No"'. *NEJMAG*, 311, 24, 1569–572.

Townsend, Robert. *Up The Organization: How to Stop the Corporation from Stifling People and Strangling Profits*. New York: Fawcett, 1970.

Tran, Ph.D., Zung Vie and Weltman, Ph.D., Arthur. 'Differential Effects of Exercise on Serum Lipid and Lipoproteins Levels Seen With Changes in Body Weight: A Meta-Analysis'. *JAMA*, 254, 7, 919–924.

Vandenbroucke, M.D., Ph.D., Jan P., et al. 'Weight, Smoking, and Mortality'. *JAMA*, 252, 20, 2859–860.

Vila, Bob, and Davison, Jane. *This Old House*. Boston, MA: Little, Brown, and Company, 1980.

Wainwright, William J. *Philosophy of Religion.* Belmont, CA: Wadsworth, 1988.

Warner, Ph.D., Kenneth E. 'Cigarette Advertising and Media Coverage of Smoking and Health'. *NEJMAG,* 312, 6, 384–88.

Wasson, M.D., Donald R. 'Substance Abuse'. *JAMA,* 252, 16, 2286–291.

West, Thomas G. 'On Education'. *Improving College and University Teaching* 28, no. 1:3–7; no. 2:61–66; no. 3:99–104.

Willett, M.D., Walter C., and McMahon, M.D., Brian. 'Diet and Cancer—An Overview'. (First of Two Parts). *NEJMAG,* 310, 10, 633–638.

———. 'Diet and Cancer—An Overview'. (Second of Two Parts). *NEJMAG,* 310, 11, 697–703.

Williams, Paul T., et al. 'Coffee Intake and Elevated Cholesterol and Apolipoprotein B Levels in Men'. *JAMA,* 253, 10, 1407–411.

Wise, M.D., Paul, H., et al. 'Racial and Socioeconomic Disparities in Childhood Mortality in Boston'. *NEJMAG,* 313, 6, 360–66.

Wolff, Robert Paul. *The Ideal of the University.* Boston, MA: Beacon, 1969.

Ziporyn, Terra. 'Latest Clue to Exercise–Induced Amenorrhea'. *JAMA,* 252, 10, 1258–263.